S O C I A L

W O R K E R S

ROBERT MULLAN

First published in 2013 by
Free Publishing Limited

Copyright © 2013 Free Publishing Limited

A CIP Catalogue of this book is available from
the British Library

ISBN: 978-1-85343-215-6

Typeset in Bembo 11pt by
www.chandlerbookdesign.co.uk

Printed in Great Britain by
Berforts Group Ltd.

It is not the consciousness of men that determines their existence, but their social existence that determines their consciousness.

Karl Marx (1859)

Advocates of capitalism are very apt to appeal to the sacred principles of liberty, which are embodied in one maxim: The fortunate must not be restrained in the exercise of tyranny over the unfortunate.

Bertrand Russell (1928)

CONTENTS

Chapter Four

Chapter Five

Chapter Six

Chapter Seven

Introduction

My final placement was based in the
CAMHS [Child and Adolescent Mental
Health Services] Team. I was involved in
a crisis intervention where 'S' a 16-year-
old female presented at CAMHS late one
afternoon feeling very depressed and suicidal.
A psychologist assessed her, where S disclosed
that she'd taken an overdose the previous
night but refused to go to hospital. The
psychologist then left, S was alone and so I
offered to sit with her until the paramedics
and her boyfriend arrived. It was as she was
leaving that she disclosed some very sensitive
and distressing information, of which I told
her I would have to inform her primary
worker and CAMHS doctor, which resulted
me in completing a child protection referral
to the Locality Team. S asked me if I could
work with her in the future, so I gained

> consent from her primary worker who
> advised me that she'd been involved with
> CAMHS for approximately 8 years and was
> very difficult to engage.

But Sue, a 27-year-old social work student, *did* find ways of working with the 16-year-old who was, allegedly, "difficult to engage with," with, it appears, positive results.

> I met with S weekly, exploring triggers to
> her self-harming and providing her with
> 24-hour information. We worked together on
> a 'positive life story album' [detailed account of
> significant events in S's life] which she enjoyed
> immensely. S was waiting for an allocated
> 'leaving care social worker' and was homeless.
> I advocated on her behalf and supported her
> by writing letters. S also became proactive
> by contacting a MIND advocate. S was
> eventually allocated a social worker and
> rehoused. My placement ended.

Sue was pleased with the work she'd undertaken, and then was pleasantly surprised by once more meeting with S.

> I bumped into S a few months ago in a
> supermarket where she told me that she was
> working in a school with children who had
> behavioural difficulties, that she'd completed
> and passed maths and English GSCE's and was
> preparing to travel the world with her brother.
> *I am so proud of her.*

This short book considers the state of social work and social work education, and its arguments stem, in part, from an account of the *student experience* - narratives and opinions of students like 'Sue' [all names, places of work and locations changed]. I have, of course, exercised what might be termed an *interpretative omnipotence*, in that through the editing of interviews with students and social workers and through the use of secondary materials, I have *constructed* what I believe to be an accurate account of aspects of social work and social work education. However, I am also aware that -to use the language of postmodernism- I have merely constructed *a particular* version of the social work enterprise (see Bryman, 2008:686). Nevertheless, I do hope that the reader finds *this* particular version compelling.

The stimulus for this book is the death of Peter Connelly (a.k.a. "Baby P") and the public reaction to it, the media outrage and, in particular, the subsequent formation of the Social Work Task Force.

The Social Work Task Force

Following the death of Victoria Climbié, Herbert Laming was commissioned by the government to instigate an in-depth investigation into child protection issues, within the wider context of social work in general. In 2003, after the *Climbié Inquiry* and the introduction of the *Every Child Matters* framework, there has been increased inspection and regulation of social workers, and the eventual introduction of a computerised Integrated Children's System [ICS]. Following the death of Peter Connelly, the government again asked Laming to investigate. His child protection review looked at the implementation of safeguarding [protection] procedures, inter-agency work, effective public accountability and developing and deploying workforce capacity. Laming reported that *many of his earlier recommendations had not been fully implemented*. His measured conclusion? "Just do it."

There was also the announcement of the establishment of a Social Work Task Force [SWTF], under the leadership of Moira Gibb, a local authority career executive. Following the Task Force's deliberations and subsequent to its Final Report, the government announced its intention to establish a new Social Work Reform Board [SWRB]. The government insisted that there would have to be "clear places on this board for the organisations which represent employers, including local government as well as CAFCASS [Children and Family Court Advisory Support Service], the NHS and private and voluntary employers, as well as for the profession, social work educators and, of course, service users" (letter from Andy Burnham and Ed Balls. Department of Health, 1 December, 2009). This Board would, in modern hyperbole, provide a 'route map for improvement.'

In the foreword to the Social Work Task Force's 2009 Final Report, entitled *Building a safe, confident future,* it asserts that its recommendations "need to be translated now into sustained action in which everyone signs up to a common purpose, and delivers on their responsibilities." The Task Force added that "social work *has arrived at a watershed moment"* (2009:1, italics added). It was intended that the aforementioned Moira Gibb would lead the reforms by establishing the Social Work Reform Board to oversee the implementation of recommendations.

In *Building a safe, confident future* it's argued that when people are made vulnerable by poverty, bereavement, addiction, isolation, mental distress, disability, neglect, abuse, or other circumstances, "what happens next matters hugely," because if outcomes are poor, if dependency becomes ingrained or harm goes unchecked, "individuals, families, communities and the economy can pay a heavy price. Good social workers can and do make a huge difference in these difficult situations" (2009:5). From the outset, the misplaced emphasis is on *social work action,* not *societal prevention.*

The Task Force argues that such "good social workers" are "confident, effective frontline professionals," who, in turn, rely on a system of "high-quality training, regulation and leadership behind them" (2009:5). Indeed the Report continues to assert that "when social workers have confidence in their own skills, purpose and identity, and in the system in place to back them up, they have a huge amount to offer" (2009:5). Nevertheless, the Task Force *does* highlight a number of problems: "At present, however, social work in England too often falls short of these basic conditions for success," because of weaknesses in "recruitment, retention, frontline resources, training, leadership, public understanding," which are "holding back the profession and making service improvement difficult to achieve" (2009:5). As a consequence, people who "look to social workers for support are not getting the consistently high quality of service they deserve" (2009:5). It is tempting to ask why the members of the Task Force -the majority of whom are involved in social work, on a day-to-day basis- did not speak out earlier?

The Report concludes by stating that it proposes a "national reform programme," to ensure "connected, co-ordinated" progress. Such reform would include better training, improved working conditions, stronger "leadership and independence," to provide a "reliable supply of confident, high quality, adaptable professionals into the workforce, where they can build long-term careers on the frontline" (2009:6). The Task Force hopes that its reforms will lead to a greater understanding among the general public, service users, other professionals and the media "of the role and purpose of social work, the demands of the job and the contribution social workers make" (2009:6). These are, of course, phrases and intentions that easily slip off the tongue, but are frustratingly vacuous in meaning and consequently extraordinarily difficult to implement.

We must remind ourselves that much of this is all too familiar.

In 1945, Dennis O'Neil, 13, was beaten to death by his foster father, Reginald Gough, at Bank Farm, Shropshire. A post-mortem examination concluded he had been starved for months and weighed just four stone. The murder trial revealed that he had sucked cows' udders in a desperate attempt for sustenance. *A subsequent Home Office inquiry identified a string of failures by the staff and agencies involved in the case: there had been confusion between the two local authorities responsible for the boy's foster placement, conflicting reports by childcare staff about his wellbeing, staff shortages and miscommunication.*

In 1973, Maria Colwell, 7, died after being starved and beaten by her stepfather, William Kepple. She suffered brain damage, a fractured rib, black eyes, extensive external bruising and internal injuries. Maria had been fostered by her aunt and uncle because her mother, Pauline, could not cope with bringing up five children on her own. Five years later Pauline decided she wanted her daughter back and Maria was returned. A subsequent inquiry by the Department of Health found that East Sussex County Council had insufficient evidence to return her to her mother, despite 50 official visits to the family, from social workers, health visitors, police and housing officers. The *Report of the Committee of Inquiry into the Care and Supervision Provided in Relation to Maria Colwell* (1974) chaired by Thomas Gilbert Field Fisher, a Recorder of the Crown Court, identified two main contributory factors to Maria's death: *the lack of communication between the agencies who were aware of her vulnerable situation, and inadequate training for social workers assigned to at-risk children.* All agencies involved in the case were criticized.

In 1987, Doreen Mason, 16-months-old, died of neglect after her mother and her boyfriend bruised, burnt and broke the child's leg, then failed to have her injuries treated. Christine Mason and Roy Aston were convicted of manslaughter and cruelty, and each received a 12 year jail sentence. Doreen was on the 'at-risk' register of Southwark Council from birth. She slept on the floor, where the couple placed junk food for her to eat. A subsequent report said her *social worker was inexperienced and given no proper training or supervision, and that Southwark social services department suffered from a "siege mentality" and of a "destructive mistrust" between senior managers.*

Perhaps more well-known was the case, in 2000, of Victoria Climbié, 8, who died from hypothermia in Tottenham, North London, after suffering months of horrific abuse and neglect. Her aunt, Marie Thérèse Kouao, and her boyfriend, Carl Manning, were both jailed for life for the girl's murder in January 2001. The public inquiry into her death began in September 2001, and led to the 'reform' of Britain's child protection services. *There were at least 12 chances for the agencies involved in her protection to have possibly saved her.*

Also in 2000, Lauren Wright, 6, was found dead after suffering a fatal punch or kick from her stepmother, Tracey Wright, which caused her digestive system to collapse. The woman was found guilty of manslaughter, as was the girl's father, Craig Wright, who had turned a blind eye to her abuse. Norfolk Social Services Department admitted it made serious mistakes and missed chances to save Lauren. *An inquiry found that inter-agency coordination was "ineffective" and social workers had not acted with "due urgency."*

Then, in August 2007 the UK media reported the tragic death in the Borough of Haringey, North London, of 17-month-old Peter Connelly ["Baby P"]. In November 2008, two people were convicted of causing or allowing the death. The court was told that Peter had been used as a 'punch bag' and that his mother had "manipulated and lied to social workers and health visitors," even smearing him with chocolate to cover his bruises. The boy was eventually found dead in his blood-splattered cot just 48-hours after a doctor had failed to notice that he had suffered a broken spine.

Reflecting on the Connelly case, Ferguson and Lavalette observe that the events were initially framed in a familiar guise: "that 'politically correct' social workers were a 'soft touch' for manipulative parents; that social workers and their way of working were, at best, problematic, at worst completely failing; that there was a need for more regulation and controls over what social workers do; that the solution was more managerialism and marketisation of social care services" (2009). However, they point out that the actual evidence contradicted many such claims. For example, in the face of the suggestion that social workers were 'failing' in their work, it was revealed that "the number of children killed has fallen steadily – down 50 per cent in England and Wales since the 1970's" (Ferguson and Lavalette, 2009). Furthermore, Britain was previously 'fourth worst' for child murders among Western nations in the 1970's, yet by 2009 it was among the best: "only four countries have fewer child murders per million," compared to America, for example, where "child murders have risen by 17 per cent since the 1970's" (Ferguson and Lavalette, 2009).

At the same time evidence has gradually emerged of an under-resourced childcare system where budgetary constraints and market methods of care delivery had made child protection, and social work generally, more difficult. As Ferguson and Lavalette assert, childcare social workers in Haringey were still working with "caseloads similar to those prior to the inquiry into the death of Victoria Climbié…[and that]…there were large numbers of agency staff working in the borough, filling gaps where people had left or were on long term sick leave" (2009). So, the evidence suggested that not only were there fewer child murders than in previous decades, social workers were working under problematic conditions with a shortage of resources and personnel. Moreover, there is also evidence that less than half of the families implicated in child murders are actually *known* to social workers at the time of such incidents (Brandon, pc, 2009).

It appears, therefore, that the public outcry over the death of Peter Connelly has obscured the fact that social work remains afflicted by the same problems which were first described by the inquiries into the deaths of Denis O'Neil in 1945, Maria Colwell in 1973, and many, many others.

There *are* problems with both social work as it is currently practiced, and the education and training programmes that produce the workforce. However, *the Task Force's response to the death of Peter Connelly is utterly misguided*. The establishment of a body tasked with reforming social work is unlikely to result in a watershed moment in thinking about social work and social work education, as what is required is a *genuine change in the prevailing social work paradigm*. Let us remind ourselves of that seminal idea of Thomas Kuhn's in his 1962 book, *The Structure of Scientific Revolutions.*

Kuhn argues that the development of science is driven, in what he calls 'normal periods of science,' by adherence to a 'paradigm.' The function of such a paradigm is to supply puzzles for scientists to solve and to provide the tools which enable this solution. A crisis in science arises when confidence is lost in the ability of the paradigm to solve particularly worrying puzzles called 'anomalies'. Such a crisis is followed by a *scientific revolution* if the existing paradigm is superseded by a rival. Kuhn claimed that science guided by one paradigm would be 'incommensurable' with science developed under a different paradigm, meaning there is *no common measure* of the different scientific theories. This thesis of incommensurability rules out certain kinds of comparison of conflicting theories, and consequently rejects some traditional approaches to scientific development, such as the view that later science builds on the knowledge produced and contained by earlier theories, or the view that later theories are closer approximations to the truth than earlier theories. *The Task Force's ideas of what social work is and could become, are incommensurate with mine.*

When the Task Force, in conjunction with the majority of tabloid newspaper articles and television bulletins, refers to 'social work' it is, invariably, talking about *child protection*. The whole of social work is reduced in this discourse to this particular area of social work practice: it is vital to appreciate that, important though child protection is, it is only *one* aspect of the occupation. For example, social work also includes -among other specialisms and areas of focus- adoption and fostering, social work in and with schools, social work with the dying and bereaved (sometimes in hospice settings), social work with older people, eating disorders work, drug and alcohol teams, adult protection, therapeutic work with children and adolescents, working with individuals who experience post-traumatic stress disorder, working within the voluntary sector, social work in the armed forces, and much more.

In his review of social work education, Nigel Parton points out that social work students make up only a small proportion of the total number of those enrolled in higher education. For example, in the years 1998/99, in nursing there were 112,307 students, in psychology 28,244, social economic and political studies 133,161, sociology 23,084, and social work 26,829. As Parton explains, registered social work students account for just 26,829 out of a total of 1,845,757, "much smaller than nursing, psychology, law and education, but comparable with sociology" (2001:168). While relatively low in number, however, he adds that "the proportion registered in both full-time and part-time *postgraduate* categories is high compared to virtually all other subjects" (2001:168, italics added). This is an important issue in terms of the attractiveness to universities of maintaining social work education, because of the higher status afforded post-graduate study and level of fee income (Parton, 2001:168).

Parton persuasively argues that poor pay, stressful working conditions and a bad press are "deterring would-be social workers from applying" for training (2001:168). Indeed, *qualified* social workers constitute a "comparatively small professional group when compared with nurses and teachers or other social care employees" (Moriarty and Murray, 2007:717-18). Compared to the total of 80,000 qualified social workers, there are over half a million teachers and a similar number of nurses. Thus, qualified social workers comprise a small segment of the "million or so people working in social care, but their professional importance outweighs their numerical size because of their statutory duties and their role as gatekeepers to other social care services" (Moriarty and Murray, 2007:718).

Social work, in its crucial and honourable role of protecting the vulnerable and disadvantaged, is far too important to be left to government, universities and other educational institutions. Nevertheless, it is precisely the state and an array of universities which determine the definitions, education and practice of social work. With a few notable exceptions, John Mayer and Noel Timms' seminal book, *The Client Speaks* (1970), remains one of the few detailed and substantive accounts of clients' ('service users') experiences of being at the receiving end of social work intervention. Similarly, very little is known about the generic student experience of social work education, other than the brief opinions expressed on the evaluation of modules and other aspects of degree courses. *This extraordinary absence of the student voice in social work education discourse* was *one* of the reasons for the research undertaken for this book. The research (2010-2012) involved interviewing first to third year students and newly qualified social workers undertaking PQ [post-qualifying] education. Perhaps it is worth noting that these students have not yet been totally transformed into *consumers of education* and therefore are partially able to see the educational process as one of discovery and debate, not simply the means necessary to acquire a qualification.

Ronald Laing's 1964 seminal book (with Aaron Esterson), *Sanity, Madness and the Family,* based on extensive interviews with the families of 'schizophrenic' women was subtitled 'Part One.' However, over the years that followed, 'Part Two' never materialised. When asked why, he described what had occurred when he interviewed so-called 'normal' families (in Mullan, 1995:281):

> Every member of the families *totally fitted*
> – getting up and going to work and going
> to school and coming back and watching

> television and doing nothing and going to
> bed…[and]…to get them to say anything
> about anything was almost impossible. They
> thought about nothing, they said nothing very
> much, they were just fucking dead and there
> was no edge or no sharpness or no challenge
> and it was very difficult to keep awake reading
> this. Just fuck all, an endless drone, about
> nothing. It was like Samuel Beckett, reams and
> reams and reams of nothing.

I would not wish to judge any of the participants in this project quite so harshly, however, it is noteworthy that quite a number of them appeared to have no views whatsoever. Issues on which one might expect students in general, and social work students in particular, to be vociferous -their education, politics, the aims and goals of the social work enterprise- elicited from a substantial proportion of interviewees a high frequency of monosyllabic responses. Conversely, it can be seen that many participants *did indeed* express strongly held, eloquently expressed observations and opinions about such issues, and their personal experiences of them.

The study adopted a qualitative paradigm to elicit rich, in-depth data, enabling a flexible investigation of the subject from the participants' perspective. A multi-method approach was adopted for the collection of both primary and secondary data, consisting of a literature review and researcher-administered interviews, qualitative questionnaires and written materials (in response to specific questions) with 60 student social workers and newly qualified social workers. Sampling was purposive, with participants identified by 'snowballing' among students at three British universities.

Informed consent was obtained from all participants, and the subsequent interviews were semi-structured and, at times, conversational and explorative. On average the interviews lasted 90 minutes or so but, on occasion, for over 3 hours.

The timing was fortuitous, in that it has coincided with the Social Work Task Force's review, in which it has elicited and evaluated evidence and, subsequently, produced a set of recommendations for Government.

Chapter One

Life stories

I was born in Cape Town, South Africa, and grew up there until I was about 8 and have lived here since. I'm the first person to finish uni in my family. I'm one of four girls from quite a big family. *I didn't have a troubled childhood, I had quite a loving family. My parents have stayed together, very happy.* I think moving around a lot is unsettling and having to meet new people built up like *resilience in me* and all that malarkey. But I think it helps me understand kids that are in care a little bit more. And like I did work in the YMCA and worked as a hospital volunteer and that's when I kind of realised, 'oh, I like working with people and I don't mind if they're a bit stinky and annoying, I still want to work with them.'

Jackie, final year student, aged 22

This social work student tells an unusual story, namely, that she experienced a *happy* family life. She moved around a lot, but says that this simply increased her resilience, an emotional characteristic which she saw as occupationally useful. Another final year student, Nicky, 33, also discussed her motivation for social work. When asked about her interests, she summarised them as follows: "I really like heavy metal and fairies and the great outdoors and camping with the children." And when asked why she decided to pursue a career in social work, she replied she "wanted to earn more money, and I wanted to improve myself and someone said that I could do it. I never thought I would be able to go to university. I got really bad grades in GCSE's. I'm not academic and I didn't think I was good enough at writing or that I could cope with the whole three-year course."

The Task Force forcefully argues that a "reformed system of education and training should begin with clear, consistent criteria for entry to social work courses -with a new regime for testing and interviewing candidates that balances academic and personal skills- so that all students are of a high calibre" (2009:7). This, of course, sounds both sensible and optimistic: but the question has to be asked – how can this be achieved? The Task Force argues that in future it would insist that the revised criteria for all applicants on social work degree courses should "include successful completion of a written test, which measures *the clarity of writing, logical coherence and the capacity for developing reflective and analytical thinking*" (2009:21, italics added). It is, however, reasonable to ask how *any* educational institution might embark on such an onerous task and, indeed, it is equally reasonable to query how such cognitive skills as "writing clarity" and "logical coherence" will be *operationalised* -for both 18 year-olds and for older students, new to higher education- and it also reasonable to ask how the *"capacity"* for *"developing reflective and analytical thinking"* will be measured.

The Task Force will also insist on "high performance" in selection interviews which will "evaluate the life and work experience of course applicants, their communication skills, creativity and emotional resilience" (2009:21). Again, it might well be asked how such elusive cognitive and emotional qualities as "creativity" and "resilience" might be uncovered and evaluated in an admissions session? Creative - how? In what particular sense? And in what context? The simple dictionary definition is elusive enough - *inventive and imaginative*. It is difficult to envisage exactly what the Task Force proposes: lengthy recruitment sessions to test applicants on Edward De Bono-type exercises, perhaps? Resilience - how will that be measured? Is the applicant simply to be asked to recount an incident in his or her own life, and the interviewer expected to assess and believe it?

The Task Force commends the manner in which the social work degree has encouraged the active participation of service users and carers "in all aspects of *degree design and delivery*...[and]...*to good effect*," and adds that, "listening to people who use services" is important (2009:7, italics added). What aspect of degree *design*? How does the Task Force know that this has been a *positive development*? And for whom? Which service users are they actually describing? - clients with borderline personality disorders? Rough sleepers? Women clients using crack and working in the sex industry, however reluctantly? Or are they in fact describing local, well-behaved and polite individuals? Indeed, in his discussion of service users and carers, Malcolm Carey has noted that a small industry has developed around *empowerment* and *involvement*, and that its "growing apparatus includes legislation, government guidance, mission statements, charters, literature, participatory projects, committees, working parties, researchers, consultants, trainers, managers, development workers and much more "(2009:186). One of his central questions is that of what proportion of service users and carers is "*directly* involved and what is being done to avoid tokenism?" (2009:186). He questions whether "service users and carers [are] permitted adequate autonomy and discretion regarding their involvement" and questions whether such involvement "seek to serve the needs and interests of service users and carers" (2009:186). Most importantly, Carey poses a broader question: "How, if at all, is participation linked to *confronting and changing* the inequitable economic, political and social structures on which participation itself is based? Is this achievable and, if not, what is participation aiming to achieve?" (2009:187).

Social work education has, generously, provided an important opportunity of "opening up professional training to certain groups that are otherwise under-represented in higher education" (Moriarty and Murray, 2007:717). Indeed, Moriarty and Murray argue that the socio-economic backgrounds of students accepted for social work training are more *diverse* than those generally in higher education (2007:724), and social work certainly is *not* the predominantly middle-class occupation it is sometimes assumed to be. Interestingly, despite the often less-than-conventional background of social work students, non-completion rates are invariably low and most students complete their courses and go on to become social workers (Moriarty and Murray, 2007:717). For example, a survey in 2001 found that 93 per cent of social work students were actually working in social work, a strong contrast to teaching, where the figure is closer to 75 per cent (Moriarty and Murray, 2007:727). However, it may be reasonably assumed that both occupations have seen a rise in withdrawal from such employment since 2001.

Holmstrom and Taylor argue that the "support needs" of social work students -particularly those from less conventional backgrounds- must be met and the "balance between support and establishing false expectations needs to be addressed" (2008:834). The belief of some in education is of a need for a 'bridging environment' in which applicants with 'potential' are admitted, "recognising the multi-dimensional nature of development that takes place during a programme and aligned with the social work values of inclusion, diversity and belief in capacity for change," and that such an approach requires acceptance that "not all who are admitted will successfully complete the programme and a commitment to a programme culture supportive of on-going development and learning" (Holmstrom and Taylor, 2008:835).

Many social work students are motivated by "a sense of idealism and altruism," and *also* significant is their "personal life experiences" (Moriarty and Murray, 2007:719). So, I will consider the biographies of the applicants, the reasons *they* put forward for their career choice, and what *they* believed were factors helpful in their education and training.

Amelia, a 23-year-old student, describes both a childhood and a motivation for social work which is somewhat more familiar that those reported earlier.

> I grew up in quite a poor area and the community is very kind of *inbred* - once you're born and you're in that community it's very hard to get out! You just stay and you have kids and then your kids have kids at thirteen in a kind of council estate way and grow up there. *I realised I wanted more.*

I wanted to come onto the social work degree and get a qualification for myself to say that I'd gone to uni *and then to make a difference* to the younger people in my area.

Q. Do you ever go back to "the community"?

Yes, and I still see sad lives with young kids living in poverty and those kids can be violent and swearing. Or, they are skanky dressed because my friends have got no money to get them clothes and things. *That's why I wanted to make something of myself.* And I thought, 'well if I did that course then, yes, I'd have the training but I would bring with it the people skills I think I needed to relate to families in crisis, to relate to especially the kind of families in poverty and with drug and alcohol and mental health issues.' *That I think can't really be taught on a course, you either have it in you or you don't,* and the course helped me to build on my academic and my legal side.

Q. So, you think that coming from a deprived background helps you in social work?

Yes, hopefully to show young people that I'm living proof, that I'm kind of practicing what I preach. 'Yes, I know you've got nothing, and there's four of you in one bedroom sharing a room and no duvet or anything, but I had that and I chose to go to school, to college, and to uni, and rose above it all.'

This account of a somewhat impoverished background and the subsequent overcoming of adversity and a determination to make a difference -especially the ability to understand and relate to the client group- was often cited in interviews.

Another student, Lorraine, in her early 30's, expresses a more pragmatic and straightforward reason for her career choice.

> I left school after finishing my GCSE's and
> went straight into working in sales. I worked
> there until I had my first child, then returned
> back into sales. Probably, all in all, for about
> 10 years. Then we moved abroad to live and
> before leaving I did a TEFL [Teaching English
> as a Foreign Language] qualification, so I could
> teach English. We lived there for around 9
> months until we had our second child, then
> returned to the UK. I had always sort of done
> voluntary work in youth clubs and things like
> that, and had wanted to continue in education
> but couldn't afford to leave work. When I
> got back to England I didn't have a job, so it
> seemed the obvious time to try and go back
> into education. So that's when I applied for
> this course.

Jenny, 33, initially describes an idyllic and happy childhood, but later in her account, clarifies the narrative.

> *I have to say my childhood was positively idyllic,*
> *unlike, I think, numbers of my colleagues.* You
> know, not quite '2.4 children' because I am

one of five, but happily married parents and
great sibling contact with my brothers. I
think if anything it made me actually think I
am exceptionally lucky in this day and age to
have such a great huge wide family that still
operates in a way that perhaps you would have
seen in the 1940's.

Having said that, my parents are happily
married, *but he is my step-dad*. My father died
when I was 6 and I was at boarding school
with a number of other forces' children
whose parents had been killed in service.
I know that there were other kids at school
who had contact with RAF Welfare Services,
so I suppose there was that on some level –
around bereavement and loss and forming
new attachments.

However, another first year student, Tracey, in her early 40's,
begins to describe a more *familiar* life story.

My mum was depressed for most of my
childhood so I just grew up with it and didn't
think anything of it. Because we thought that
was *normal*. My dad worked away a lot. *My
mum wasn't motivated enough to make us do what
we had to do. Emotionally she wasn't able to give
us the kind of support that maybe we wanted.* All
that has given me an insight into possibly what
families or young people in the community
can face.

The student was asked why she was no longer a nurse, her previous occupation.

Just before I got pregnant with my oldest child, I worked on a ward where there was quite a constant high level of depression and verbal aggression directed towards staff. The team wasn't very supportive of each other nor was management, so I got a bit fed up with it really. So after that I worked with the elderly. Then when I had my last baby, I just gave up…[pauses]…you know, there's a saying with psychiatric nurses, 'which one is the patient and which one is the nurse?' Well that's very true [laughs]. When I trained there was, in my experience, as many problems on *that* side of the bed as there was on the other.

Less-than-happy childhoods

James, a final year student, recalls his formative years in considerable detail and exemplifies a familiar set of experiences and beliefs that tend to be found in a considerable number -perhaps the majority- of social workers: disinterested or dysfunctional parents; childhood illnesses or trauma; an interest in working with people and working to promote social justice.

I'm 43. I'm a chef, I've been a chef for 20 years and I'm a good chef! I've worked all over the world. I was really ill as a kid and I kind of drifted into catering because its hours

were good and you could go to work *drunk*.
You could get drunk at work and nobody said
anything! And there were lots of women! Win
win win!

Q. You were ill as a child. With what?

I was diagnosed with cancer [Hodgkins]
when I was 10.   First time was fine - six
months in hospital. Then, in the mid-seventies
I was put on the men's cancer ward, so I was
surrounded by 60-year-old men dying of
cancer. That pretty much happened every year.
The fourth time I had loads of radiotherapy
and at that point they said, 'we can't give him
anymore radiation, it will kill him before the
cancer does.' Consequently, I was one of the
first people in the UK to have *chemo*. As
you can imagine, there were no drugs for the
side effects or anything like that, so it was 18
months of hell. My whole life I had grown up
being told, 'next time you're ill you're going to
die.' Consequently, *live fast, die young* [laughs].
So I went out and had a lot of fun. My
alcohol and drug use was always to enable me
to have more fun. It was never a crutch.

James was encouraged to speak about his family life.

My parents were shit. Now I don't have
anything to do with them. I spoke to my
father last year for the first time in 8 years,
because my sister tricked me into it.

Speak to my mother on an annual basis, I
suppose. They weren't awful, don't get me
wrong, they were just a bit self-absorbed.
Because of my medicinal needs, I was stuck
in a hospital 50 miles from home and I'd get
visited once a week, once a fortnight. So there
was a lot of distance involved for long periods
of time. [They were] classic kind of 'rubbish
parent,' hard to prioritise their needs over
those of their kids. I stopped running away
from home at 14 'cos I figured I only had 18
months before I could leave legally, which I
did - soon as the chemo had finished.

My mother, apparently, is the youngest of 7
of a mixed-race marriage. Her mother was
Indian and wanted a boy, so my mother was
treated like a skivvy. Apparently she had a
breakdown, never loved by her mother. My
father is the son of hard-working Shetlanders.
His father used to catch whales in boats with
sticks. Literally, *literally*. He was pall-bearer at
Scott of the Antarctic's funeral. Lost toes in
the Antarctic with him, fought in the Spanish
civil war. Lots of interesting stuff, but not
really a family man.

Q. What about your education, your school life?

School was horrible. I got dragged to Wales
just after I was diagnosed the first time,
10-years-old, to the arse-end of Wales. Tenby,
Saunders Foot - I was up in the mountains,

the nearest telephone box was a mile and a
half away, as was the only street light. I was
English, so I was an outsider straight away, then
I got ill, so I was a 'freak.' Then they found
out my nan was black so I was also the local
'nigger,' so that was fun [laughs]. I spent a lot
of time in and out of hospital, so I missed a lot
of school. I wasn't obnoxious, but I knew what
I wanted and if I didn't think something was
relevant I wouldn't really pay attention. I was
the only boy in the school that did cookery.
Everybody else went off and did woodwork
– 'what do I need to go and chop up bits of
wood for? I'm leaving home in 18 months, I
want to learn how to cook.'

Q. So tell me about your catering career.

I was running a 5 star game lodge on
the banks of the Zambezi, just outside of
Livingstone, and I was driving back one
night…[and]…there was an eagle owl on the
road, big bugger, so I dipped my lights, and
I'm going round this big sweeping bend on a
road I knew really well. So I'm doing about
70, round this bend avoiding the potholes,
I'm on dip, and the big eagle owl flies away
and I'm half way round and I don't bother
putting my lights back on main beam because
I know where I'm going. Anyway I flip the
lights back onto full and there's three elephants
walking down the bloody road and I spin it. I
haven't got the seat belt on so I come through

the windscreen and I'm crushed as it's rolling
down the road. Spend the night in the bush
because nobody knows I'm there, waking up
coming to consciousness, trying to crawl to
the road just in case there's a truck driving by.
Then get found by a local Zambian electrical
engineer, who picks me up and puts me in the
back of his pickup truck and takes me to the
police station.

Q. How much damage did you do to yourself?

Obviously I have done certain amounts of
damage [laughs]. They take me to the hospital
in Livingstone, which is rubbish – 'he's got
a broken arm.' My boss turns up, with his
massive first aid box. Then they get a private
ambulance, take me across the border into
Zimbabwe, to Victoria Falls. Then they get
me in an air ambulance and fly me down to
Harare. Died essentially – on the table in
Harare, both lungs collapsed. Spent 7 weeks
in intensive care. I had broken my back in
3 places, and I bust nearly all ribs, shattered
the base of my skull, completely crushed my
whole right shoulder.

Q. And this was when?

That was 1998; I had bog standard
backpackers' insurance. The company I was
working for actually stumped up all the fees,
agreed to fly me home. So they flew me

first class, Zimbabwe Air, back home - but
essentially they just dumped me at Heathrow.
'The NHS will look after me now.' There's
me in my wheelchair at Heathrow, kind
of like, 'what the fuck am I going to do
now?' My sister put me up for a week, but I
couldn't handle it, so I headed straight back to
Brighton and had a job a week later, chopping
up in a pub I knew. They used to help me
up the stairs and put me on a stool. I was
homeless and had no money.

Q. And then?

I got better slowly but it was quite a social pub
which was why I'd drunk in there in the first
place. I knew them quite well and as I got
better I spent more of my money on beer and
did more and more *cocaine*. Ended up running
one of their pubs and I did that for about 3
years until I was kind of well enough and in
the right place. Then I was offered a business
deal, a franchise at a university, running all of
their bar food. I got to the end of it and I
hadn't made any money and I was like, 'fuck
this, I've had enough of cooking, I want to
do something else.' I had always kind of felt
I wasn't stupid, but being in an environment
seeing all these dumb fuck 18-year-olds
walking out with good degrees, doing nothing
for three years but party and shag, I thought,
'I can do that.'

Q. So, you decided to leave the catering industry?

I've always been a boring bastard as far as
kind of social justice and people's rights are
concerned. I like people and I believe people
are inherently good, most of the time. And I've
always believed that but put off by the route –
you have to get a degree. Then there's the other
side of the coin: *what job can you walk into with
no experience where that lack of experience is deemed
to be good experience?* Social work I think is one
of the only jobs where you can say, 'well, I have
been a tosser most of my life.' Oh, *'excellent!'*
That's seen as a good thing. Kind of like rehab
workers, isn't it? Drug users, come through the
system, then go back and work there as workers.

So, I'd made a decision – *'social work*, I think
I'd be good at that. Okay, the bureaucracy
I might have a bit of trouble with, but as far
as real social work goes, I can see me doing
that.' Then it was figuring how I was going
to get there. There was no way I could've
walked into this course 'green,' academically,
so I had to go off and do an access course. I
also needed some experience and spent a year
doing bits of voluntary work here and there.
So I did the access course, which was really
challenging, because you're in a room with a
bunch of people and everybody's intimidated
by the whole education thing. Everybody
thinks they're a failure to some degree because
they're adults who've failed in education.

This student endured many personal and emotional problems both in childhood and later life: a seemingly ambivalent set of parents; a childhood wracked with illness, painful and relentless treatment, and possible impending death; an education punctuated by adverse reactions from peers; possible alcohol and drug dependence, and a career that ultimately brought frustration and a lack of satisfaction; and finally a life-threatening accident. This was the stuff of James's life which ultimately brought him to his career choice - in particular the sense of social justice which developed throughout his life and the belief that his *own inadequacies were good training for the job*. Indeed, this calculation -weighing up the advantages of personal problems and possible empathy, against the possibility of being *too* damaged to deal with someone else's issues- is central in the evaluation of the motivation of many social work students.

In an interesting piece of research, Jane Vincent considers the possible 'unconscious motivation' involved in the decision to pursue social work as a career. In her overview of the field she notes, unsurprisingly, that, as in "nursing, gender is an important factor in social work, where, despite recent changes and an increase in the number of men entering and managing the profession, women are still a significant majority, at least in the lower grades of qualified and unqualified social workers" (1996:64). She considers that this orientation towards caring for others, "may be rooted in a biological disposition to mothering" and subsequently reinforced by societal norms and the unconscious relationship between mother and daughter, which can result in "women undertaking a social role as caretaker and nurturer of others" (1996:64). Certainly, the statistics confirm the demographic trend: *that at the lower and middle strata of social work, women dominate*. It is only at the more managerial levels that men begin to emerge in significant numbers.

Vincent's research-based hypothesis is that social workers may well have endured childhood experiences which *unconsciously* influence their choice of profession. Her sample demonstrated that 42 per cent of social work students experienced significant separation from one or both parents: 23 per cent from mother, 26 per cent from father and 13 per cent from both parents. She asserts that this "seemed to me a remarkably high percentage and may perhaps indicate a link between early separation and the choice of social work as a career" (1996:67).Vincent adds that it was obviously impossible to indicate whether this was because the early loss of a parent leads to "pathological mourning in adult life," expressed as a result of unconscious dynamics with the remaining parent who seeks a partner or parent in the child, or whether, at a more conscious level,"the child has to take on new social roles and tasks for practical reasons, such as supporting a working parent by looking after younger siblings" (1996:67).

Interestingly, Vincent surmises that many social work training courses, "in their efforts to encourage open access and equal opportunities, have dropped from their admissions process any detailed attention to conscious and unconscious motivation in their applicants." She adds that, unlike psychodynamic counselling or psychotherapy training, social work training does not require personal therapy, "and our own personalities and pathologies are not acknowledged as part of our learning and development during the course"(1996:67). Significantly, Vincent argues that those individuals who have not had their needs met in childhood may have difficulty acknowledging and attending to their *own* neediness. As a consequence, they may end up "powerfully identifying with the neediness of others, or projecting their own neediness into others and feeling persecuted by the other person's demands," and hoping somehow to resolve their own neediness by attending to the needs of others. Importantly, Vincent argues that such individuals "find it impossible, in today's crisis-oriented and statute-driven practice, to get anything satisfying back from their interactions with service users." This failure may then be compounded by a "lack of nourishing supervision or by unsatisfactory relationships in their personal lives, so that the end result is sickness and burn-out" (Vincent, 1996:67-68).

Certainly, in this research project I found overwhelming evidence of the affinity between childhood -and indeed adult- emotional disturbance *and* a subsequent desire for a career in social work. Consider the following students who were raised in so-called 'reconstituted' families, as a result of some kind of marital discord or familial break up.

First, a final year student, Kelly, in her late 20's and a single parent.

> I am registered blind, with a guide dog. I have one child and live in rented accommodation. *What brought me to being here where I am today, I guess, stems from my childhood. Well, I had incidences with a step-parent where she was quite violent to me. I remember making a disclosure at school and social workers got involved.* Then my step-mum said to social workers that actually the bruises and injuries I sustained were partly me walking into things. It was done with basically no follow-up given. So I felt let down. I got into a lot of trouble for saying to social workers that I needed help.

Kelly was asked whether violence was a *significant* feature of her childhood.

> Yeah, I'd say from the age of about 3 until about 8 or 9. I think what stopped it was I began to become aware that what she was doing wasn't right. But it's a very complicated story. On a more positive note, when I was a little bit older, about 16 and I lost an element of eyesight and I needed some quite intensive rehabilitation work to make me more confident in going out and living as much of an independent life as possible. *That* side of social services was amazing. Really *empowering.* I'd go so far to say I wouldn't be here today if it wasn't for that kind of support I received in my teenage years. *So my motivation to being a social worker is to kind of mend the negative areas that I felt as a child.*
>
> I was one of 8. I was the single step-child to that particular female. So I wasn't her biological child, but the other 7 in the household were. My father was the biological father for 5 of us. So he had me, and she already had two, and then they married and had more children.
>
> *You know I wanted to change the world and I think the degree has told me that that's not possible.* But that's the kind of person and personality I have. I want to do the best for anyone, and if I can help in any way I will.

We returned to the earlier discussion of her initial dealings
with social workers.

> It was a teacher who'd commented on my
> bruises, so I spoke to her and then a social
> worker spoke to me. But I think the 'let
> down' came when they went straight out to
> speak to the social worker involved and I was
> told nothing. I think the first I heard was my
> step-mum saying, 'oh, we had social workers
> round, you're in real trouble.'
>
> I was at logger heads with my step-mum and
> dad. Big long story, but I found out that my
> real mum had been in touch for about ten
> years but her letters had been hidden. I found
> them when I was 16 and then didn't want
> anything to do with my step-mum and dad.

Trish, another final-year student, 29, also recalls a troubled
childhood although, unlike Kelly, she had no subsequent
experience of social work involvement.

> I grew up with my mum. My dad walked
> out, I think, when I was probably 18 months
> or 2. I say I grew up with my mum, but I
> actually spent most of my time with my nan,
> because my mum worked days and nights to
> pay the rent and put food on the table. It was
> a happy childhood though, there was nothing
> bad about it. *I didn't know my dad until about 5
> years ago. I class my dad now as my step-dad and
> my step-dad is now my dad.* He came onto the

scene when I was about 4, I think. We lived
with him and he's always been my dad.
I've got a half-brother, Josh, who I class as my
brother. And then my real dad has got three
sons who I'm now in contact with. And my
step-dad, because my mum and he split up,
he has got two little ones with another
lady [laughs]!

Q. So when did all the 'troubles' begin?

Well, my mum had a miscarriage – I think it
was a miscarriage or perhaps it was a stillbirth,
I can't remember. It was 1990 so I would've
been 10. And everything went a bit wrong
from there because of the way that mum and
dad were after the miscarriage. They sort of
pushed me out a bit and I spent a lot of time
at my nan's while they sort of got over it.
They didn't really talk to me about it. So I
started rebelling a bit from then. And then my
mum got pregnant with Josh, and he was born
three months premature and was in hospital
for three months and mum was literally
travelling up there about 3 times a day. So I
was at my nan's most of the time then. I was a
cow really, took it all out on my mum and dad
and then I lived with my nan permanently.

Q. Did your mum work at all?

My mum was a nursing auxiliary with the
district nurse team and also did night duties

at residential homes. My nan has always
worked in residential homes. So I remember
as a kid, going with my nan to these places.
So she was working in social care, and she'd
spoken to me and said, 'oh I think you would
enjoy it.' I thought, 'ok, then, let's give it a
go.' So I applied for the job and got one in
Adult Services.

Of course much of this is unsurprising, given the profound
changes in family structures and household size over the past
four decades. These changes are worth noting, given their
central importance to the fabric of social work intervention.
Since the various legislative and social changes, emanating
from the 1960's -the *Divorce Reform Act* of 1969, which
introduced the 'no fault' principle; the introduction of
the female contraceptive pill; the strengthening of *some*
women's rights; the introduction of labour-saving domestic
appliances- there have been what can only be described as
seismic changes in family and household structure:

- Statistically, two fifths of all marriages end in
  divorce (and such numbers, note, do not include
  the number of *separated couples* or indeed those in
  destructive or unfulfilling relationships).

- 4 out of 5 couples now *cohabit* prior to marriage.

- 6 million adults and 10 per cent of all children
  live in so-called 'reconstituted families,' that is,
  families formed from the remarriage of one or both
  partners.

- Remarriage is less successful than a first marriage. In 1900, 90 per cent of all marriages were first marriages, but by 2010 that figure had dropped to approximately 50 per cent.

Perhaps most indicative of the numerous changes in family and household is that of the *tripling* of the number of 'one parent families,' from 4 per cent of all households in 1971 to 12 per cent in 2010. And, households consisting of only 'one person' have doubled in the same period from 6 to 12 per cent.

Of course the issue of 'one parent families' -invariably, but not exclusively, families led by *mothers-* is one that is politically and socially divisive. Despite some reports and opinion to the contrary, there's little evidence to suggest that such families are formed for the primary purpose of, say, acquiring social housing: a more likely explanation is that of individual ill-education and male irresponsibility. Indeed, a more disturbing and long-established trend is that of young men -some black, others white, very few Asian- abandoning parental responsibility. It is perhaps unnecessary to repeat the obvious conclusion that for some boys and, to a lesser extent, girls, living without a father in the household *and in a life of material deprivation*, will quite possibly lead to entry into a social world of crime, inclusion in the criminal justice system and, most depressingly, lead them to repeat the behaviour of their absent fathers, abandoning the children *they* create.

Lucinda, a final-year student in her late 30's, another single parent, had to deal with wider family responsibilities in addition to raising her own children. She too had childhood contact with social workers.

My family was part of a stepfamily because my mum had me on her own then met my step-father who already had two children. He'd actually got custody of his two children so we lived together as a family. However, his ex-wife decided to cause quite a few problems and obviously that reflected on our family life. Hence, me and my step-sister ended up with a social worker when we were about 4, until we were about 5. This lady [social worker] used to come into school, which was lovely. We used to go out and have picnics and make pipe cleaner dollies and that sort of stuff. *Yeah, my family was quite -not dysfunctional- but disjointed through most of my growing up.* I didn't really get on with any of my step-sisters. Then there were additional children to the family and I suppose when I was at school, when I was sort of 14 or 15 and had to look at options, my thinking was to go into some sort of caring profession and I actually went back to school to do a vocational qualification which entailed going to a nursery and a nursing home.

Q. You said that your step-dad's ex-wife caused some problems for you. Can you elaborate?

My step dad's ex-wife had quite severe mental health issues and was actually admitted to hospital quite a few times. We lived in a small community where she used to post things all round the village and she just used to cause mayhem. And it was sort of understandable,

because she'd lost her children, even though
she still had contact.

My dad was quite flippant and kept saying, 'take
no notice,' which obviously doesn't help when
my mum's at home all day with three children
under the age of 5. And that's how Social
Services got involved, purely as a duty really,
and from what my mum's told me -obviously I
can't remember an awful lot- they made these
visits just to appease his ex-wife. They didn't
suspect we were in any danger.

Q. Okay, tell me about your education.

I've been in education now for five years,
starting when I was 33. I did my access course
in 2005. Prior to that both my nan and my
dad had been terminally ill, so while I'd been
at home looking after the kids I'd spent a lot
of time caring for them as well. Which sort
of made me think about nursing. So I did
the access course, but while I was there I just
thought, 'the more I read about nursing, there's
too much personal care really.' And then I hit
on the idea that actually, I'd quite liked my
social worker, and I like people, and it's a way
of doing something caring, so I applied for the
social work degree.

Initially, I was going to do it because I wanted
to work with older people. Purely because
of working with dad and nan, and trying to

sort out their care. I did a lot of the practical
stuff for them, taking them to appointments
and things like that. And that's what got me
interested and thinking, 'how do people who
are at home in this situation manage?'

Q. Did you have any other offers of a place on a degree
course, other than here?

When I was interviewed here I felt they
wanted to know more about *me* and about
why I was interested in doing it. The
interview at the other university was far
more academic. It's got a fantastic library. It's
beautiful - if I was 18-years-old, fantastic,
I wouldn't have thought twice about going
there and utilising everything they offered.
But I've got kids, I needed to come to
university, do my lectures, and then get home.

Eric, in his 30's, and a rare breed -a *male* student social
worker- describes being raised in a single-parent household,
but with the consequence that the *strength of his mother*, he
believes, created in him values of caring and fairness that
propelled him into his chosen career.

East London boy originally, come from a
very working-class background. Although I
didn't know my granddads -they died when
I was very young- I kind of lived under
their shadow of being *dockers*. My mum was
pregnant at 15 with my sister, in the very late
60's, at a time when there was a lot of social

stigma around and she was made to leave by
my nan -which was quite strange, because
they was [sic] very close- to get her own place
once the baby was born. That was at 16. My
dad was very young as well, 17, and it was a bit
of a shambles marriage really.

My mum was the biggest social worker in my life
and that's where I really looked at a lot of this
values stuff, because you know *when we are
talking about social work it's all about values*, that's
what it is. Skills, you can pick up.

I grew up in a very mixed council estate.
Ended up living predominantly in Hackney.
*My mum left my dad and there was a complicated
situation where I was left with my dad and my
dad -for no reason of his own- didn't really know
how to be a dad.* I was separated from my sister
and spent about 6 months living with my
dad and his girlfriend who was 21. I kind of
remember that being quite a difficult time for
me personally, until, eventually my mum came
and got me.

Q. I presume *you* didn't become a docker?

I started off in a bank. It was a clearing house,
which was like a big head office and then
progressed a little bit to being eventually a
small league kind of 'team leader'. Ridiculous
titles that they give you. Couldn't stand it. I
took voluntary redundancy from there and

didn't know what to do with myself. Did
bits and pieces and then I worked in a Vidal
Sassoon salon, because my sister works there
and absolutely loved it. It was the time of my
life. I loved it because as much as it is a very
shallow industry, I learnt to have fun.

Q. Any personal relationships at this time?

Yes, had my first serious relationship then.
My first girlfriend was from 'up north' and her
dad was a rugby league pro in the 80's and very
working-class. She had a very good upbringing,
private school, and I started seeing these
things that I'd never seen before. *Eating out in
restaurants!* It still makes me laugh now. This
idea where you sit and have your dinner where
there are all these other people watching you.
I still get a bit strange over that now [laughs]. I
started seeing these other sides to life and then
ended up going travelling because I'd become
really interested in how people *lived* and quite
interested in who *I* was at that age.

I sat and had a conversation with an Australian
fella in Thailand and we were just having a
general conversation and he was telling me
about Aboriginal people. I kind of related
to him because he spoke about them being
'disconnected from society' and I felt that too.
On leaving, as I got up, he just said to me, 'you
should be a social worker.'

The following students are more specific about marital and family breakdown. Firstly, Marion, a final-year student in her late 40's, discusses her troubled marriage and what she terms her 'blended family.'

> I have a large blended family. Got three step-sons, a son and two daughters, and grandchildren. I come from Shepperton in Middlesex. I met my first husband on holiday when I was 18, foolishly got together with him, then spent just over 20 years with him. *It was a very controlled marriage.* That ended and I actually met my second husband only two months after I got rid of the first one [laughs]. Not literally got rid of as, sadly, he's still living up the road from me. But the second husband is much better.

> I'm 48, 49 this year in July. Before I met my first husband I wouldn't have had any reason to have anything to do with social services. Didn't have anything to do with benefits, had a very good childhood, very good parents, a nice safe upbringing. Met my first husband, who wasn't very good at working, he came from a family whose work ethic was quite poor. They were all quite used to being on benefits. In fact, he spent about 15 years of our marriage on benefits claiming to have a bad back. He wouldn't let me work, wouldn't look after the children. *Then my oldest son got involved with drugs, developed mental illness -paranoid schizophrenia, which was diagnosed as drug induced- and then he committed suicide.*

Q. When was that?

> I started work in October 2003 and he killed
> himself in November 2003, so three weeks
> after I started the new job. I was working
> with children with special needs in a school
> before that, and got fed up of the importance
> being on whether they can understand that 5
> and 5 made 10 or what this word meant, and
> all I was worrying about was, 'what happens to
> that child when they go home tonight?'

> I was also dealing with behaviour issues. They
> would come in in the morning and I'd try
> to settle them into school ready for the day,
> and when I was going home from work I
> was wondering, 'what sort of weekend is such
> and such a child having, what is their step-
> dad doing this weekend?' because there was a
> problem with the step-dad. Quite a physical
> man. In the end I thought, 'I can't do anything
> to make a difference here. There are plenty of
> other people in this school who want to do the
> maths and the literacy, actually I want to know
> what is happening to these children *socially*.' So
> that's when I made the change.

Q. Does anyone else in your family have an interest in
social care, social work?

> My elder sister looks after a man with severe
> learning difficulties and before that she was
> working with adults with learning difficulties.

My mum was a nurse. So, yes, caring is within
the family in one form or another.

Adeela, a 22-year-old and first year student, born in Pakistan
but now settled in the UK, offers a revealing account of an
unsuccessful arranged marriage and also the deep seated
reasons for her career choice.

I was born in Pakistan and brought up in the
capital, Islamabad. I have a brother *who was born
blind* and a younger sister. In my house, even
though my brother was older than me, I was
the responsible one. I was caring about him
because he was my brother. I grew up with
him and I was going to school with him, and
taking him to the mosque. Caring for him all
the time without even realising it. My mum is
very religious and she prays. My father is totally
the opposite. He gambles, he drinks, he does
everything. He was working in Dubai as an
engineer, and he started his business and that
didn't work out and then he couldn't come
back because he owed so much money to
people. So we ended up living without him for
seven years and without any support. So, that
was difficult. And then I finished my college
when I was 18 and I got married [sighs].

Q. An arranged marriage, or a semi-arranged marriage?

It was a traditional arranged marriage and I
was a bit shocked because I never thought my
family is 'that kind of family' who traditionally

arrange a marriage for you – because
although my mum is religious, the rest of the
family is not. You know, we have freedom to
go to universities, college; I mean my aunties
and uncles all went to universities and colleges.
I was the youngest person in my whole family
to get married at the age of 18.

Q. And your husband?

He was born in England and was older than
me. I was 18 and he was 30. And he went
back to Pakistan and got married to me and
then I came over here and that was a big
transition, leaving my family.

Q. Sounds like it was a big shock.

It was a shock because I thought they were
going to engage me, which is very common.
You know, you get engaged at 18 or 19 and
you get married when you are 20-23. I felt,
'my parents will give me time to finish my
studies and everything.' But my gran said,
'no, because the boy wants to go back, and
they don't want to take time they just want
to get married, because he doesn't like it here'
[Pakistan]. And I thought, 'well if he don't
like the country, why the hell is he marrying
me?' We are about to start a family, he has
to come back, my family is here, his family is
going to be here and obviously we are going

to have children at some point. And I said to
my mum, 'what are you doing?' And she was
like, 'look you have to see, your father is not
around, it's very hard to get a good spouse,
they're a good family.' *I remember seeing him at
the wedding. I think that's the first time that he
saw me.*

Q. So what happened then?

I came to England. That was a big culture
shock, because when I was growing up my
thought was that western countries are more
educated and more optimistic about life
[laughs]. Yeah that was a good dream!   I was
expected to just do the housework and not
question my husband, even when he wouldn't
be around me. I was like, 'okay, what is going
on?' and I said, 'you don't communicate with
me, you don't spend time with me, you have
no intentions of doing anything like that, what
is going on?' He would say, 'that is the way I
am and you have to deal with it.'

The women and men *are so far away from their
culture, here*. Back home, they would question
things but then they have family networks and
friends to share their thoughts and support
them *emotionally*. When you get *here*, you're
just by yourself. You have to think, 'I have to
live with these people for the rest of my life
and I don't have any support network, so I'll
do what they say or I'm stuffed.'

Adeela was asked how her family reacted to her problems. Did they know she was struggling?

> The thing is, you don't discuss these things, because it's not really 'ladylike' to discuss your personal life in my circles. You just deal with it. You know, 'everybody goes through it, and be a housewife.' 'At least your husband isn't drinking,' and I'm like, 'why would I marry someone who drinks in the first place, and why would you make me marry someone who drinks?' Whenever I discussed this matter with any of my family they would say, 'you are too young to understand, you will get on with it, but you have too much age difference and then culture difference.' I would say, 'you lot put me in that position, fix it.' But then they say, 'no, it is *your* marriage, *you* fix it.'

Q. So, what did you do?

> I was like, '*you* fix it because you put me in that position. I am putting up with it for five years, I don't have any friends, I'm not allowed to meet friends, I'm not allowed to go out much.' I *did* go to college because obviously they couldn't deny me that. Because I was like – 'I am staying home and he don't [sic] want to have children either and what do I do, staying home all day and listening to your mother, I am not going to do that. I have to work and I have to go out and get my life.' And most of all I wanted to be *independent*.

So my parents said, 'yeah, yeah, that's fine,' and
then he said, 'yeah it's alright,' but I also said to
my parents, 'you have to talk to him and talk
to his family.' When my parents started talking
to his family he said, 'fine, I'm not putting up
with it and I have nothing to do with you, so
you can leave the house.'

Given the conventional Muslim context, Adeela was asked,
'if he didn't want children, why did he want to get married?'

I have no idea. You know this thing is killing
me right now to get the answer, but that's the
problem, *he won't answer me.* See, you know
that he has that *control* and when I try to talk
things through he makes me feel that it's
always *my* fault and it's just that I don't like
his family.

We then returned to her motivation for a career in social
work.

When I was with my brother and growing up,
I always wanted to help people, and because
my mum is quite religious, there was that
aspect as well. She was always doing charity
and she always put people first.   Even though
she don't [sic] have money she would give it
to people. *That is how she brought us up, you
know, just think of other people more than yourself,
and I would think that's crap, but then that's how
she brought us up.*

Then I was talking to someone in the Asian
circle and this girl -and her parents were
really, really strict Muslims, and were from
Bangladesh- she said to me she was molested
as a child and her parents wouldn't believe her.
Molested as a child by her uncle. I was talking to
her a lot and she was quite depressed because
her brothers were doing whatever they want
to do, they were having girlfriends they were
going out, going to brothels, *everything.*   So I
thought, 'you know, there are lots and lots and
lots of people who are just stuck and want a
better life, and if an English person tried to
help them out the only thing they would say
is, "oh well, they have become westernised
now. English people are just brainwashing our
children."' They won't see the actual point
or the problem, they just see some different
colour person or outsider invading their
territory. So that motivated me.

Christina, in her early 20's and in the process of completing
her course, also refers to family dysfunction and the terrible
consequences that followed on from her parents' divorce.

My parents divorced when I was 7, then for
two years I was almost completely anorexic. It
wasn't labelled that, I just didn't eat. And so
childhood wasn't great for me. I still don't
really like children and I think that's maybe
something to do with it.   But at home I had
to grow up really fast, because it'd just be my
mum and she kind of lapsed in the parenting

role as soon as my parents divorced. It was very much like, 'get your own school lunches, your own washing, sort yourself out.' I have always been a bit more responsible and have been told I've thrived on responsibility and that's the kind of person that I am.

I moved out when I was 16 and lived with my boyfriend. He made me throw away the prospectuses for everywhere else and said I couldn't do it [the social work degree] anywhere but *here*. I actually broke up with him in the August before I started here. So it was irrelevant in the end [laughs]. Plus, when I came for my interview I felt really at home here. *The buildings kind of felt familiar and homely, like I had been here in a past life or something.*

Q. So what was your first year like?

I had depression in my first year, I was kind of aware of it, struggled a bit through the year. I got counselling over the summer up until Year Two. Started anti-depressants and things and then tried to come back and just couldn't. My tutor was absolutely amazing: I went to him and said, 'look, I'd feel sorry for somebody if *I* was their social worker and I don't like that.' He made me feel more than welcome to return and I think that made a big difference.

Finally, a first year student, in her early 20's, completes these accounts of the adverse consequences of family disorder, although she doesn't consciously relate her childhood difficulties to the decision she made to enter social work.

> I'm from Cornwall. Both my parents are from London, neither went to university. I have an older sister who went to university straight after college. I went to college, although I don't think I particularly applied myself there. Couldn't be bothered to be honest. Moved out of home when I was 16, so pretty much just got drunk all through college. Didn't take it seriously; fell into a job, working with people with autism and through that then moved to Ireland. Came back from Ireland, then worked with adults with learning disabilities and did a modern *apprenticeship* in health and social care. Basically an NVQ, key skills and extra bits. It was nice to be learning and exercising my brain again. And then I decided to go travelling for three months and that's when I started thinking, 'what can I do with my career now? All I can do to progress is become a manager,' and I didn't want to be a manager, so decided to look at doing a social work degree.

Q. Can you tell me a little about your work with people with autism?

> I enjoyed working with them, and I enjoyed the environment where I felt I was *supporting people*. I did some work with elderly people but I didn't like the caring side, I liked the

supporting side. *I like to empower them to do it for themselves. To me that is what social work is all about.* The other thing about social work is that you are constantly training and that really enticed me, because I want to keep learning.

My parents got divorced when I was younger. *I went to counselling for a year because I reacted quite badly.* I was 8 at the time. I went to see a child psychologist. I started destroying things because I didn't like the fact that my parents had split up. It wasn't explained to me particularly well, and there were also issues with my neighbour at the time. But I wouldn't say anything particularly inspired me, and none of my family work in the care industry or have anything to do with social work.

Previous contact with social workers

Another motivational factor for a number of students, unsurprisingly, *is actual contact with social workers when as a child or young adult* (which has already been referred to). Two quite different accounts follow. First is Leanne, completing her course and aged 22.

My family is my mum, my sister and myself. I was the first person in my family to come to university. *I'm Jewish.*

She was asked how she would describe her family.

If you look at it sociologically -going on my
mum's current status and income- in theory
we're *underclass,* because she's on benefits, ill
and stuff. But then, on the other hand, I went
to a private secondary school, so I guess that
would be middle class. *My dad divorced my*
mum when I was six and I've not had any contact
with him since I was 12 or 13. I just know he's a
policeman. I haven't heard anything else because
I have no contact with him. My nursery was a
private nursery, my primary school was private
and my secondary school was private and
then I went to a public college when I was
16. My nursery and primary were Jewish. Was
Batmitzvahed at 12 or 13 and then I taught
after that at the sunday school. Then I ran a
Jewish youth group. I *have* had a crisis of faith
when I thought it was all just a pile of crap,
but I've come back to it.

We discussed Leanne's mother, whom she describes as,
"ill and on benefits."

Because my mum's not very well with her
mental health, there were always issues around my
mum raising me and my sister, so social services were
involved with my family from when I was a young
age, until I was about 14 or 15. We had some
really, really shit social workers, but we had
one social worker in particular who I thought
was really, really good, and I used to look
forward to him coming round. He just used to
make things easier and he *understood.* I think

that, if he hadn't have been involved in my
life, I don't think I'd be where I am today. *I*
think I would be a lot more screwed up and I think
if he can do that for us then I guess that's one of the
reasons I want to be able to help others.

Leanne was asked to clarify what she meant by "shit social
workers."

Lots of things; they never bothered turning
up, they didn't call to say they weren't turning
up or were going to be late, and that used to
irritate both me and my mum. They were often
quite blunt and quite rude, never listening,
never wanted to know what *our* opinions were.
And very, very quick, to place blame without
looking into the reasons behind things. Like, if
something had happened and my mum had hit
us or something, they were very quick to place
the blame but wouldn't consider the fact that
my mum wasn't mentally well.

Q. And the "good social worker?"

I think he made himself -I don't know if it's
the right word- *accessible* to us. He came
down thinking-wise to *our* level. He wanted
to get to know us and wanted to help us. I
don't know what the word is -*prosper*, I guess,
and do well- and I don't know, he was just
a really really nice guy and I think that you
could see he genuinely cared.

Q. So he inspired you to be a social worker?

To be honest I kind of decided on being a
social worker when I was 13 or so, and then
I moved away from the idea for a while and
looked into going into physiotherapy or
nursing, and I'm not sure whether that was my
own choice or because my mum didn't want
me to be a social worker because 'that's too
dangerous' and she worried I'd get stabbed or
something. But I sort of came back to it: it's
a typical cliché thing, *I think I wanted to be able
to help people*, specifically kids with disabilities.
I didn't necessarily want to do it from the
physical hands-on side of things like physio,
which I think I would have enjoyed, but I
wanted to do it more from - I don't know,
more *life changing type things* and social work is
kind of a way into that.

I came into social work quite naïvely, because
the only experience I've had of social workers
myself, was in the *long term*. I don't know
what you'd call them - but children in need,
childhood protection, like the long-term
teams. You know, where I would stay with my
social workers as a kid, I got to know them
and they would take me out and we would go
to the park and we would go for ice cream,
that sort of thing. So, naïvely, I think I came
into it with that sort of idealistic view of what
a social worker was and I guess it has changed
now to reality since I've gone into placements.

It's kind of a harsh reality really, *you haven't got the freedom to do what you want and to help kids how you want to, you are constricted by time and resources and the boundaries of where you are actually placed.*

Q. You did some voluntary work, didn't you?

Yeah, I did voluntary work in two different family centres and it opened my eyes to estate life and how rough people can be. I know it's a horrible thing to say, but it's the truth, you know, because I hadn't really come across that before. *I also think being Jewish has helped because I try not to discriminate against others, because I have been discriminated against myself.* I got bullied for it through secondary school because I was the only Jewish kid at school. When I was at primary school I remember there was a psychiatric home up the road from us and a guy used to walk down every day and shout 'fucking Nazis are going to come and kill you all,' and at primary school age, that was quite scary. I went for a job interview once and all was going well and somehow religion came up into it. I quite happily sat there and said I was Jewish, and instantly the lady changed towards me and I didn't get the job.

Izzy, in her early twenties, is a survivor from a problematic childhood and with experience of social work contact as a child.

I grew up on a council estate with my mum
and three brothers and sisters.   My mum
married three times when I was younger. *I
had three dads, one after the other.* Me, my older
sister and my younger brother all had the same
dad. My little sister has got a different dad and
then my mum married again and he semi-
adopted us, as his. Mum was a single mum. *I
ended up being the mum*, because my sister was
quite erratic, my little brother and little sister
needed looking after, so I used to look after
them. If they were having problems at school
I sorted it out and I was very protective of
them. I was the most sensible one. Always
been, ever since I was tiny, I was *always* the one
who was looking after everyone else.

Sometimes there was no money, but when
there *was,* my mum was very creative with the
money she had. I don't think we were very
materialistic because we didn't have anything.
Because of the places that I lived and the
people I hung around with, I think a lot of
people who had problems tended to migrate
to me, because I was quite protective and I
was quite strong willed, quite steady and
level-headed.

Q. Can you elaborate?

Well, I've always worked with kids even when
I wasn't working with them, if you know what
I mean [laughs]! I did theatre with the juniors

and I ran the intermediates at one point, just supporting them to learn the skills. I was always good at the whole mediation thing between adults and kids, because I could see both points of view and I could sort of like build the relationships up with them. Basically, a lot of the adults used to shout at the kids at theatre and I would be like, 'that's not the way to get them to learn something, it's supposed to be fun.' So I would work with the kids to try and get them to see the adults' point of view.

I wanted to be a single mum at 16. That was what I really wanted to do. I really thought my mum was ace, I thought she was really a very smart woman and she worked really hard and she was a good mum. She gave us *time*, she didn't just give us money and stuff.

Q. Men?

I didn't really have much respect for men, apart from my granddad – but he didn't stand up for himself, so he wasn't a very strong male role model. My mum was very good at –like in our teenage years– bringing male friends home. Not in a boyfriend context, but she had a really good social network with a lot of males who she wasn't dating and there were quite a few strong characters in there.

With my background you did see a lot of social worker involvement and stuff. My friend *always*

had social workers and we had them involved
with us twice. Once was with the contact
thing with my dad and with supervised
contact, and that didn't work out very well at
all. The second time, my nan decided she was
going to report my mum because she wanted
to adopt me - *not the rest of them, just me,*
because I look like her, and my mum went nuts.

I didn't like social workers until I came *here.*
We had quite a few problems with the fact
that they didn't do their role properly. Like
they didn't read the file or they didn't believe
what was written in the files. *They cut corners*
and they made mistakes that could have been really,
really dangerous - we were having supervised
contact and the social worker used to just leave and
not be in the room.

Q. What did your mum think of your career choice?

My mum said, 'you're too naïve to do it.'
You know what she said to me -an awful
thing to say- she said, 'you're going to go
away travelling and end up having a kid with
a black man who is going to go back to his
country with the kid and you are going to
be devastated.' And I was so mortified that
she had said it, I was like, 'this is completely
inappropriate, absolutely outrageous.' But it
was more that she didn't realise I was my own
person and I could think things through and I
was very aware of the dangers around.

Unsurprisingly, the recurring themes throughout the interviews were of childhood disturbance, emotional uncertainty, the sense of loss, an equal sense of 'not belonging,' and, importantly, a desire to help others, 'make a difference,' and possibly try to combat social injustice.

Chapter Two

Students: age, gender, race, 'suitability'

> Honestly, I think the standard of the students
> who were selected for the course wasn't good
> enough. I think people underestimated how
> academic the degree was going to be, so I
> don't think the academic ability was there.
> But also there was *the age of students*, which
> was an issue. It's a degree you're now allowed
> to take at 18, but I think it's an exceptionally
> difficult job to learn from a book and if you've
> no life experience, whether it be positive or
> negative, I think you're on a sticky wicket.
>
> *Debs, 43, first year student*

For the past few decades the stereotype of the social work
student is that of the 'mature student,' the politically motivated

student, perhaps the religious or morally committed and, much less so, the *younger* student. In the past, the courses such students have taken in order to qualify in social work have been a mixture of non-graduate and graduate diplomas. However, in 2001, the Department of Health announced that the basic qualification for social work would become an *undergraduate degree*. According to Orme et al., this was a response to "political and public disquiet about the perceived quality of some social work practitioners and reductions in the numbers of social workers qualifying each year as well as being part of the government's wider aim to modernize the social care workforce" (2009:162). The previous professional qualification in social work, the Diploma in Social Work (DipSW), had been in existence for some ten years and had often been criticised "for its *competence-based* approach" (Orme et al., 2009:163, italics added). The new curriculum was, to some extent, left to the discretion of the individual programme providers but there were specifications that core subject areas had to meet. To an extent the *new* curriculum was not that dissimilar to the old one, with the usual pot-pourri of academic modules -social policy, sociology, developmental psychology, and values and ethics- along with more 'practical' modules, like the protection of children and adults, and the so-called 'skills' of social work.

One of the consequences of the 2001 change was the increase in younger students, often at the expense of more 'mature' applicants. Indeed, traditionally, as Parton argues, "the majority of applicants to social work courses have been in the age bands 25-34 and it is mature students who have been most severely hit by the government's funding reforms" (2001:169). In fact, the figures for enrolments to higher education institutions by the over-25's decreased by nearly a quarter between 1995 and 2001, with the two biggest falls in 1997 -the year New Labour was returned to power- when applications were down by more than 6 per cent, and in 1998, when applications fell by almost 13 per cent (Parton, 2001:169). Certainly, the overall trend of an increase in applicants under 21 and a decrease in applicants over 40 is confirmed by my small sample: for example, in 2008, there were 28 students under the age of 21 and a mere 11 over the age of 40.

Nevertheless, as Moriarty and Murray point out, overall there's a striking age contrast between social work courses and other courses: half of those accepted for social work are aged 25 and over, compared to a mere 10 per cent of all other UCAS admissions. As they point out, this is in "keeping with previous work showing that people tend to apply for social work *after* experience of paid employment in social care or an unrelated occupation and is in contrast to teaching or nursing where the UCAS Annual Datasets and the annual reports prepared by the Graduate Teacher Training Registry and the Nursing and Midwifery Admissions Service show that applicants for teacher training and nursing are more similar in age to the majority of students in higher education" (2007:723).

What led to the significant decision to alter the age criterion in social work? Since the 1950's the idea has been to attract 'mature students' into social work education and training, as it was believed such candidates needed some *care experience* or *life experience* prior to training. However, according to Social Care Institute for Excellence (SCIE), the age criterion only came down to 18 "when the new age discrimination legislation was in preparation, as part of the new equalities bill" (pc, SCIE, 2009). However, this is only part of the explanation. Under the previous professional social work qualification, the two-year Diploma in Social

Work (DipSW), students could not qualify until they were aged 22 or over. By 2003, such age restrictions had been removed and the new three-year degree course could be taken straight from school or college. There is now *no age below which a person cannot qualify*, although in practice, university acceptance rules mean that a student will not begin such a course below the age of 18 and therefore not qualify before the academic year in which they are 21. According to the Department of Health (DOH), the General Social Care Council (GSCC) was responsible for this decision and, the DOH comments that "it is difficult to comment on the reasons for the change. *One factor appears to have been that age was no longer felt to be an appropriate way to distinguish suitability for social work,*" as it was "felt that aptitude, training and qualifications were the appropriate factors to take into account when deciding whether a person was suited to social work, rather than their age on qualifying," and that it was "also felt that the removal of the age restriction might encourage more students to come forward from younger age groups to train as social workers" (pc, DOH, 2009, italics added).

Of course an additional factor, in more recent decades, is the almost obsessive determination by New Labour and to a lesser extent Conservative-Liberal Democrat Coalition governments to aim for a 50 per cent enrolment in university education for those eligible to do so and, at a stroke, conceal ever-increasing youth unemployment. Therefore, invariably, social work, like other subjects, has recruited individuals who *might* not have held prior enthusiasm for social work, social work education or indeed *any* education, but rather felt *compelled* to enter higher education.

In its Final Report, the Social Work Task Force welcomed the introduction of the undergraduate degree in social work, asserting that, "with increases in the time spent by students in assessed practice, [it] was a very important development for social work. It heralded the arrival of a graduate profession"(2009:15). It argues that the degree "has also achieved its aim of continuing to attract a high proportion of students from different black and minority ethnic groups, helping to ensure that social workers represent the diverse communities they serve" (2009:16). Significantly, and without citing specific numbers or statistics, they *claim* that the new degree has also "succeeded in *increasing the proportion of younger candidates and school leavers into the courses, while maintaining high levels of mature students*, thus opening up the possibility that all those who have the potential to become good practitioners can do so, regardless of age" (2009:16, italics added).

Yet the Task Force has misgivings, having "heard from many sources" that initial education and training is not yet "reliable enough in meeting its primary objective, which must be to prepare students for the demands of frontline practice" (2009:16). Employers claim they are unable to appoint newly qualified social workers (NQSWs) because of a lack of suitable applicants. At the same time, some NQSWs cannot find jobs and some NQSWs are "often expected to take on unrealistically complex tasks because of the acute recruitment and retention problem in many authorities," so, according to the Task Force, "employers need to be realistic about the time people need to progress from achieving a professional qualification to operating as a full professional, and what therefore a newly qualified social worker should be asked to do" (2009:16).

Age on entry to social work education

Age on entry to the undergraduate degree course was an issue discussed by *all* the participants: whether or not younger individuals could properly or sensitively or effectively train as social workers; whether chronological age was effectively correlated with 'maturity'; and whether or not older students had some *added value* and were better suited to the occupation.

Firstly, the students recall their initial impressions of their peers. Sandra, an older student in her late 30's and in her final year, recalls the first day of the course.

> I remember the first day we had to go into
> one of the big lecture auditoriums, and we
> were asked to stand in a line, running upwards,
> according to our ages. I was quite shocked
> that I was one of the oldest ones [laughs]! But
> I saw that there were a lot of young people.
> That was also a shock, but then I knew the age
> had been dropped and I knew that years ago
> it was 25 and that it'd been dropped to 18. So
> I didn't *not* expect that. As far as black people
> – a very, very, small minority. To me it almost
> looks like it's a token, you have to have two
> or three black people to keep in with equal
> opportunities. There were quite a few people
> over the age of 30 though, which was quite
> nice. *I felt quite comfortable because I didn't feel
> like I was too old to go back into education.*

Q. Can you talk about the younger students?

The younger students don't actually ask
questions – very few questions, anyway. You
tended to find that the young people all stuck
together, probably because they'd all been out
clubbing the night before. Then you also had
the *sponsored students* who also stuck together.
The black people also stuck together. And
you had that for the whole three years. The
younger people tended to be more studious
in lectures, and they'd write masses of notes
all the way through lectures, even though
you were given handouts with pretty much
everything you needed to know. Whereas, I
suppose, *I just used to sit back and listen.* I do
find the older students tended to ask more
questions and seemed less afraid to ask them.

Q. Can you imagine being a client and meeting one of
these younger student social workers?

*I've come across people while I've been doing the
degree that haven't been impressed with having very
young people turn up at their house.* Actually, in
my first year, I remember going out with a
social worker to a young girl who had a child
of about 2, and where there were domestic
violence issues. She wasn't saying anything to
me originally, and then at one point I said to
her, 'don't worry, once she gets to play school
it'll be sorted out,' and she sort of looked at
me and said, 'oh, do you have kids?' It was
probably the first time I thought, 'well, how
much information do I divulge about myself?'

But I have actually come to think over the last three years that I don't mind if there're snippets of my life that people know about, if it helps them in some way. To let them realise that I'm as normal as they are. *I mean, you hear so many people who've had social workers, who say to me, 'oh bloody social workers, you get some young girl turn up who knows nothing, they've never had children, how would they know how to bring up kids?'*

Karen, 43, a first year student, was even more critical of her peers. In particular she ponders the issue of bringing adverse or traumatic childhood experiences onto the course.

It appeared to me that there were a number of people that were on the degree for the wrong reasons. They'd either had involvement with social workers, when they were younger, and were kind of determined to change the profession from the inside because they'd had poor experiences from social workers. In itself this isn't *necessarily* a bad thing, but I remember being in seminar groups and the issues that they'd experienced as children or as young adults were still very *undealt with* [sic]. It was almost as if they were using the degree to try and resolve them, and you can't do that. *You shouldn't.*

She was asked about the younger students.

There were only a handful, maybe -I don't know- seven or eight that were around the

18 mark. *But they were like rabbits in headlights, almost from day one.* Actually from the first time we had a social worker who came in to speak to us -which was very very early on in the first year- they were rabbits in the headlights: 'Oh my god, what on earth have I got myself into?' because of the kind of reality of what social work is like, you know, that it's not fun and games.

Another older student, Anita, also in her early 40's, also discussed the age range.

I was surprised that some of them were so young. I think that was probably the only thing I thought: young ones, and this is a job which I know will be quite hard going and you may be having to make a judgement about someone's life and would that person have enough experience to be able to make the right decision about them?

Q. So what kind of age group of students were you expecting?

Not necessarily as old as me, but maybe more mid-twenties - I was kind of expecting that kind of age group. There've only been a couple of times when they [younger students] have irritated me, in as much as when you've done the work and they've done absolutely bugger all. But my theory is that I'm there for myself and if you do group work it *is* irritating,

but I'm there for myself, so if they don't want
to work, then that's up to them.

Q. You're a parent: do you think that's important for
the work?

Being a parent? I don't think it's important,
but I think that it gives you a bit of an
extra insight into how families operate
and the possible problems they encounter.
I don't think it's important because everybody
has been part of a family, haven't they? Well
everyone has problems, don't they?
I suppose like nursing, social work attracts
people who have encountered problems in
life and might appreciate how hard life can
sometimes be.

Questioned about the specific issue of age on entry to the
course, Becky, 25, a third year student, recalls the first days
of the course.

My initial reactions? That some students were
very young. That they looked *very young,* as if
they were just out of school really. I thought
people would probably be older. *Obviously
there are some people on the course that I still think
are too young to be social workers.*

Q. Why?

Just their attitudes, their reactions I guess to
certain things. The way they *talk* about things,

I don't know…[sighs]… just some people - if they knocked on my door and said, 'I am your social worker,' I would be like, 'bye!' Maybe not everybody. But I personally would be like, 'who are you to tell me?' especially if it was a visit to a home to speak about their children. I would be like, 'what experience have you got? Who are you to tell me how to bring up my children?' But then I still think that about myself, because I don't have children, and I just think I might have to tell people how to bring up their children and I haven't actually got any children myself. So who am I to tell them?

I think the age to begin a social work course should be 21. 18 is very young, especially for someone who has just come out of school, haven't really done anything else. It's just been education all the way through. I think you need to go out and get a bit of life experience to be a social worker.

A first year student, Linda, 48, expresses a similar opinion.

Some of them I thought, 'mm, you're a bit young. What life experience can you have?' Which is really judgmental, but I have to admit I still feel 18 is too young to start this course. At 18 I would've *known nothing* [sic], I would've had *no life experience* and I would've been completely naïve. But that's just how I think and it's probably not a very fair thing to think. They're not *all* airheads at 18 [laughs].

But some of them, I have to say, some of
them I still feel *are* airheads, while others have
definitely matured and come along.

Emma, a student in her mid-20's, perceives the issue somewhat
differently, and provides a more nuanced observation.

Everyone was like, so smart and everything.
They had all their folders and looked really
organised and we all carried our files and stuff
making us look like students [laughs]. And
it did feel like you were a student, and it was
quite a cool feeling actually. I liked going to
lectures, and although everyone used to moan
about one of our lecturers in particular, I
actually really used to love sitting in lectures
and listening.

We've got quite a vast age group. I did feel
very young because some of the older people
did make me feel a bit young, sometimes.
But actually, that was only in the first week
and when we did that line up of 'youngest
to oldest' I was actually very surprised that I
wasn't the youngest one, which was really nice.

Q. What about *after* the first few weeks?

I think it's been shown over the three years
we've been here that some of the younger
students have got *vast experience for their age*.
You know, they've come from backgrounds
that've given them a real adult way of looking

at the world and a real, very sensible level-
headedness, and *I don't think age matters, I think
it's the personality that you are. I think it's the
experience you've had and where you are in your
life.* If you can do all that self-reflection, and
you can hold your own and you have the
confidence to go with it, and *that empathy
which you can't learn*, then I think you'll do
well. But then you've got some older people
who actually haven't got any of that and it's
the younger people who've got all of that.

Emma discussed further such 'life experiences.'

I think there were [on the course] some
people who've come from a background
where they'd probably had social work
involvement. But then there were people that
you couldn't imagine ever having any social
work involvement, you know, like the 'old
middle classes.' I wouldn't say that with *all* the
working class people I thought, 'oh, they've
had social work involvement,' but I think
there's that sign that some people actually *have*
had involvement *because they still carry it.* You
can sense a mark on them, that they've had
social work involvement. *There're a lot of people
on the course who've had difficulties in their lives
and they haven't moved on and they look like they
need support and help.*

Q. Do you think that is why some people do this course,
because they need help?

Yes. I think because they need help they don't want to focus on their need for help, they want to focus on somebody else's, *and I think fixing other people's problems can make you feel better about your own.* And I think people make that mistake, but unless you can deal with your own issues, I think when things get really challenging, you're going to break. *I think it's quite difficult to manage problems at home and problems at work.* I think they'll make good social workers but not yet, not in this stage of their lives. Not take it personally as well, because you're going to get people who are horrible to you - professional people, people you're working with, service users and also your colleagues. They're going to challenge you, you are going to have times when you think the world's against you and it's too much.

Q. Were there many students like this?

In the first year I thought there were quite a few people who needed to be sorting things out at home. That first year was challenging emotionally, because you're reading a lot of stuff, and you're learning a lot. Like the child protection training, that really did affect quite a few people. Although it *should* affect you, you should also be able to keep going, it shouldn't break you.

But I also think that lots of the younger people have chosen this course because they don't know what else to do. I don't think it's been particularly thought through: maybe they've done childcare and they don't really want to work in a nursery, so they think, 'well, maybe I'll do social work.' And I don't think a lot of them really knew what social work was about.   For example, we were discussing Baby P and the tutor was reading out what'd happened, and also about Victoria Climbié and you know, obviously everyone finds it very upsetting, but I think having to go outside and cry was a bit much. I think if you know you're going to be working in this area it's going to be something you have to deal with.

A male student, Daniel, in his 30's, and in his final year, also expresses his own particular view on the issue of 'age.'

I hear some of these conversations going on in the canteen between students and I am a mature student and initially I did think, 'what on earth is going on?' We've got these very young, predominantly girls, kids who look like they've just come out of school. Although these were my initial thoughts, and I kind of cling on to some of them, it's interesting how I *now* see it - because there're a lot of young girls where the age *isn't* apparent.   I've got to know some of these young girls and, yes, I would still say I do question whether they are ready for social work practice. That's not

to say that they can't be social workers in
a particular area, I just think - what's the
perception of service users? Now *even I* have
been looked at as 'too young' on occasions and
I kind of wonder about what it must be like
for *them*. In terms of practice I don't know,
I'm not here to judge - but from what I see
in the class room, they are not ready. *Many of
them*. It's about maturity really, not about age
so much.

Jenny, 23, continues the theme.

The only time I spoke up -*I never tend to speak
up*, but I did in one seminar-   was when we
were talking about Christmas presents and the
importance of buying things. I said, 'I don't.' I
never grew up with lots of presents, it wasn't
an important thing for us and I was just telling
a story which was hard because everyone was
looking at me, and then someone interrupted
me and was like, 'well you wouldn't
understand because you're not a parent.'
And she didn't know that I'm *not* a parent, I
could've been a parent, she doesn't even know
me. I was just like, 'wow,' I didn't know what
to say back, because I was like, what do I say to
that, that I'm not a parent?

I think it depends what line of social work
you're in. Like, I've been in fostering for the
last nine months and I've not really had any
problems. But I think if I was in front line,

child protection work, every day you would get, 'you look the same age as my child,' kind of thing.

The lecturers put us in groups, *but it's always the same people who talk.* And I know there're loads of people who've got really good things to say but they don't get the opportunity. There're two different sides to it, aren't there? Either, they should speak up more or the people who talk a lot should talk less.

Finally, Tess, 24, speaks on behalf of younger students.

I've always been quite grown up and mature for my age. But I think having the work experience *does* open your eyes a lot more, and gives you an insight into people, compared to some people on the course, like the younger ones who have gone school-college-uni. Academically they are very, very, clever, and you can see that they understand how to write essays. You *can* kind of tell the people who have worked, being that little bit more mature and a little bit more talkative.

Q. Your first impressions?

I thought there were quite a lot of older people, like kind of my mum's age and there were quite a lot of people who looked quite a lot younger. I did honestly think they [the older students] were brave for doing the

course, their kids may have grown up, or they
may not have had kids and they wanted a
career. And I thought, 'good for them' to be
able to do that, because I know, if someone
said to my mum about uni now, she wouldn't
even consider it. And there were some very
young students, who I thought might struggle
on placements.

I'm sometimes very aware that I'm younger
and *look* younger, and I'm aware of the opinion
a parent would have on that, especially when
I'm giving advice or support. So the people
who look younger than me, I think, it's just
the first impression: if you were to open the
door as a service user, and have one of them
[younger students] approach you, would you be
consciously aware of their age and think, 'well
do they know this, this and this, and will they
understand about taking my child away if that
is the case?' Because they wouldn't have had
children themselves. Also there were less [sic]
men on the course. I thought there would've
probably been an equal balance.

Q. So, what *is* the right age for someone to start
the course?

*I think you need an age range of sort of 23 and
above to start, just so you can get the work experience,
or just to live your life outside of being at school
and college, just to suss out how things are and the
world of work.* [And], yes, on first impressions

there were people who did look more 'upper
class' than what [sic] I did, and over the course
a lot of that has been taken away and I kind of
see everyone as the same. There's probably a
handful, maybe four or five, who I still think
are very kind of snobby and up their own arse,
and, for whatever reason, will stay that way in
practice. *And there're a handful on the course who I
think are in the wrong profession.*

Sponsored students

One of the consequences of many local authorities failing to
recruit or retain social workers is that for the past few decades
some unqualified social workers have been sponsored and
attended courses, paid for by their employer. In return, and
once qualified, these sponsored students are contracted to
work for the employer for a specified number of years.
These students enter the degree course invariably knowing
far more about the roles and responsibilities of social work
and local authorities than their peers. They are also often
older than the majority of the other students on the course.

Lynne, 21, a final year student, discusses sponsored
students.

When we started they all seemed so much
older than me [19] and because I've always
looked quite young anyway, they all looked
so much older than me. It's not really been a
problem, to be honest, although there *was* a
bit of a problem, I think, half-way through
our first year when some of the older people

said they didn't want to be taught with us
younger ones because we didn't have the right
experiences. But as the course has progressed
some of the *sponsored students*, not all of them,
some of them, they've become more snobby.
They've got high opinions of themselves and
most of them seem to value *their* opinion
above anyone else's. Always put all of us down,
especially us younger ones or people who've
got obvious problems. They will pick on us
more - 'you don't know what you're talking
about,' and all this sort of stuff.

Malak, a first year, is also unimpressed with the sponsored
students.

We have lots of *sponsored* students which I
personally don't like [laughs]. They know
it all! And they expect you to know it and
they come here like a *worker*, not as a student
to learn. It's a work thing for them, it isn't
a training for them, they're not here to
understand and explore. When I speak to the
majority of them they, you know, 'we know
our job, and they want us to do this degree so
that we can be qualified social workers.' I was
like, 'did you not listen to yourself? You're not
qualified and those people are not so stupid to
spend that amount of money on you to come
all the way to university because you already
know your job. That's why they're sending
you.' It really upsets me, because they think
they know it all, but they don't. They know

their job but they don't know the *idea* of social
work and what social work is about.

A first year student, Eleanor, in her late 20's, recalls the first
day of the course.

> *I was surprised at how many mature students there*
> *were and also surprised at the number of young*
> *people.* Probably surprised at the spectrum of
> people. Disappointed there weren't more men:
> it is quite disappointing there aren't more men
> in this line of work. And *class*, yeah, I would
> say they were all fairly middle class I suppose,
> but some of the younger ones, possibly not.

Q. What about the sponsored students?

> I do find the *seconded* [sponsored] students are
> a little bit 'know it all' and I think that presents
> some problems on the course. *Because they*
> *know so much, sometimes the tutors will speak to*
> *them and forget that we don't actually know what*
> *they're talking about.* Particularly when it comes
> to legislation and stuff, the lecturers will talk
> about this section or that section, but we might
> not fully understand, whereas the seconded
> students can relate to them a lot more.

> I think everybody has got their own little
> groups, and I think they *do* provide some
> support for each other. I'd say that the group
> *I'm in with* give each other a lot of support.
> *We're quite happy to read each other's assignments*

and talk through questions and things we have
concerns about. Perhaps there are some people
on the course that don't have that support. I
think the younger people, they're the ones
who leave it to the last minute and perhaps are
more like fish out of water.

Sam, in her late 20's, and a first year, also recalls her first day.

What am I doing? I was surprised at how
many young people there were, because I
was led to believe that you had to have some
sort of life experience and I was worried
that possibly *I* hadn't had enough. So I was
surprised at that. *I was also surprised at how*
many people had come into it that were already
doing the job - and said that they are doing the
same job, and were seconded, and just doing this
degree in order to get a pay rise. Shocking!

Nicky, a final year *sponsored* student, in her late 20's, paints
a more optimistic picture of her peers.

I was really excited actually and thinking,
'right, okay this is it now, oh my God!' Yeah,
I was feeling that this is the start of something
completely different. You know, I'd have never
have dreamed I could come and do this and
I'm gonna [sic] meet all these different people
and I'm gonna [sic] learn so much and I'm
gonna [sic] be a different person when I've
finished it. I thought how different all the
people were. All the different ages: looking at

some of the younger people and thinking, 'how are they going to cope with some of the work that social workers do?' That was mostly it. On the first week I was a bit overwhelmed by all the information that was thrown at us, and I did feel really, really, tired, but determined to go home and read through all of it [laughs].

She emphasised that despite her extensive experience she still believed she was still learning.

We're still in a process of learning as newly qualified social workers. You can't just go out there and do the job, just like that. I think they're still going to be picking up experiences, just like everybody else, so they'll get better at their role just like everybody else will, possibly at the same rate.

When we first started and we were doing social policy and other modules, I really struggled with some of the things people were talking about. Well, people who come to university are all middle-class and have got money or have got a good education. Single mums from a certain town, you know, they're the ones that need social workers, and that came up a few times [laughs] and I felt quite strongly about that.

Q. Because you were a single mum from that town?

Yes, and I'd sit up and say so.

Men in social work

In social work, women outnumber men. Indeed, in the 1980's, men comprised almost a third of social work students, whereas they are now less than a fifth and "the combination of a decline in status and comparative levels of pay have differentially impacted upon the number of men applying to be social workers" (Moriarty and Murray, 2007:718; also see Mahadevan, 2009). However, what is *also* true is that male social workers are more likely to experience greater career *progression*.

In one university in this sample, for every dozen female students, there is one male. In the academic year 2008-9, the actual figures were 38 female and 3 males. These statistics conform to the norm. For example, according to GSCC statistics, of those *currently* studying for the BA in Social Work only 14.4 per cent are male, i.e., 2060 compared to 12,198 female students (GSCC, pc, 2010). And of course, in terms of *qualified social workers*, the figures are broadly similar; of the 82,850 registered social workers, just over 23 per cent are male (GSCC, pc, 2010).

There are several potential factors impacting upon the likelihood of men entering social work, including "important socio-cultural factors such as perceptions of role and gendered stereotypes; financial and household finance/ responsibilities; the public image and status of social work and the separation of probation and social work education and training as well as negative public images regarding male student/social worker motivation" (Holmstrom and Taylor, 2008:826-27). And, of course, it seems reasonable to assume that these factors also impact upon students whilst actually studying, affecting both their performance and experience of training and education.

James, a final year student, discusses his gender and other peer issues.

> Well, I always knew, as well as one *can* know,
> that coming in *as a male* I was going to be in
> the minority. But I was quite surprised by
> what a striking minority that was.
>
> There was an incident in the first year when
> one of the more senior members of the group
> made a complaint that was actually leaked:
> they thought the group should be split in
> two, and all 'the children' should go off in one
> direction and all the adults in another. This
> tickled me because that's a real social work
> attitude isn't it [laughs]!
>
> *I was surprised how ignorant and how naïve an*
> *awful lot of people on the course were.* I think
> I was expecting a bit more from my fellow
> students. Again, this is not the most racially
> diverse area in the country. I was expecting
> it to be predominantly white, predominantly
> middle class, bigoted and ignorant, and I got
> what I expected.

Meera, a first year, recalls her initial perceptions.

> I was shocked, because I remember going
> to the auditorium where all the social work
> students were, and I was sitting next to my
> colleague and I turned around and, like there
> are only a few -no actually one, two, three-

men. Why? And I think, if it's a really tough
job, first of all, why're men not doing it, and
why are they all women? Then I thought,
maybe it's just our university which has so
many women. But then when I'm doing my
placement, I'm realising they're all women
everywhere! So what's going on? Is it like,
I don't know, is it a less paid job, is it? Or
maybe people just think that social work is for
women to do. But I was really shocked, *really,
really shocked*.

Liz, 22, also noticed the absence of males in her first year.

Well, we had like 3 or 4 males in the first year,
compared to the rest of them being females.
Personally I think there's [sic] not enough
men in social work. I genuinely believe there
is [sic] not enough. I couldn't comment on
how the selection process goes on the degree:
I can only assume that you didn't have many
males apply because it's certainly a very big
imbalance to have, what, 35 females and 4
males? I think that male social workers are
just as essential as female ones.

She expresses, perhaps, a somewhat naïve view of 'class.'

I guess if I'm honest, I thought a lot of the
younger ones, who were quite naïve, and quite
closed about issues like racism and things, were
very cushioned in their upbringing. I'd argue
that maybe they were more the 'upper class

younger people.' They've been very protected
-which isn't a bad thing- just very protected
from the real world. I truly believe that you
need to be quite wise about the world and
things that go on around you to do a good job.
*Initially, yeah, I didn't think that they'd be as good
at it as I was or people like me would be.*

Q. In terms of age?

Yes, in terms of age, but also in terms of
experience. I mean, I could compare myself
to some of the 19-year-olds, and I think at that
age I was still a little bit more streetwise than
they were, but that's probably because of my
turbulent childhood.

Another 22-year-old, Debs, also a final year student, recalls
the male-female ratio.

To me, social work has always been a *mixed
profession* in my experience and when I did
voluntary work in social services, there were
always men and women. *I guess looking at most
caring professions, men aren't there but they do seem
to be at management level.*

Becky, a third year, 29, is somewhat more pragmatic.

They always say at work, that it's always good
to have a guy on the team, because it sort of
diffuses the team, sort of mellows it more than
all these girls - *chat, chat, chat.* I don't know,

really. I think it's just nice to have a male
point of view as well, rather than it just being
the female side to it.

Final year, Nicky, agrees.

When we're having discussions, it's good to
see things from a male perspective, to have
that – and the power differences, when
there's a big group of women it can be very
overpowering, I think, for a few men [laughs].
But then, on the other hand, I think they quite
like to be nurtured and looked after. *Having
worked in social services, I already knew that the
amount of male social workers is very low, yet the
amount of male managers is much higher [laughs].
Interestingly enough, in mental health there seems to
be more male social workers.*

Finally, Bob, a male student in his early thirties, and in his
final year, turns the issue around.

This might sound a strange thing to say –and I
don't know what it says about me– but there's
a *manliness* about the men on this course.
They're still very much men, and maybe
that's my assumption about what social work
is: in terms of representation it needs to be
addressed. What attracted you to this course,
why are you here? Why do you think men
are *not* here? What do the women think?
What do the black men think? These are all
conversations that are all relevant.

Racism on the course

Given that one of the central values of social work should
be that of holding a *non-judgemental* attitude, it *might* appear
surprising and disturbing that a number of interviewees
discussed racism on the course.

In terms of national recruitment, and using UCAS
acceptance data, Moriarty and Murray report that "social
work has been comparatively successful in attracting
black applicants" (2007:721), as well as "older applicants,
applicants with non-traditional educational qualifications
and applicants from routine and semi-routine occupational
backgrounds, all of whom are currently under-represented
in higher education" (2007:721). The authors argue that
the proportion of black people accepted for social work is
among the highest for any subject, although Asian people,
people with disabilities and men are under represented
(2007:722-23). This sample confirms this: of the past 3
intakes of students, and out of an average class size of 40, only
3 have been ethnic minority students. It might be worth
noting that *students with disabilities* are "even more under-
represented in social work than they are in higher education
as a whole" (Moriarty and Murray, 2007:724). It is assumed
that some selection practices -for example, time-limited
exercises for people with dyslexia- and also problems with
practice placements, act as possible additional barriers to
such students attempting to enter social work education.

Jonah, a final year student, recalls his experiences of
racism on the degree and in social work itself.

> I was raised in Uganda. I was shocked because
> on the course there were just two of us [later
> 4] who were black students. We took a taxi

here, and then walking around the campus we
couldn't see any other black students. And
actually not even on the campus, *in the town*,
you couldn't see anyone.

Racism can happen in many ways, as you
might know. First of all it started when we
were beginners, you could see people were just
neglecting us. We used to sit, four of us, lunch-
time, break-time, tea-time, we just used to sit
together, talk about things, like our experience
of being new students in this 'strange' place.
Then you could see other students, they were
a bit distant, except for a few who wanted
to come and interact with us. Where we felt
there was an element of racism, was when it
came to lectures, discussions and things - you
give your idea or your opinion, maybe basing
it on African culture or African background,
but you feel it's not being taken on board. It's
been an issue all the way through. There was an
example: in Africa, we get smacked, that's the
way they discipline us. So my black colleague
was trying to raise all these sorts of issues, and
she was trying to say that because Britain is
now a multicultural country, you might be
a social worker working with a black family
and you might not know this [children being
smacked as a way to discipline them]. Other
students weren't interested in that.

*I've been put in a group and some other student
didn't want to work with me.* Then there're other

people who don't want to listen to my ideas. It
does shock me, because having gone through
all that training and actually listening to what
we're being told, I wonder what people like
that are doing on this course?

Another ethnic minority student, Miz, in her first year,
comments on the issue.

I was surprised because when we started
university and I was away from my family
and it was *Eid*, I was like, 'right, I need to find
some Asian students or a Muslim to say, "oh,
by the way it's *Eid*."' I was like, 'we don't have
any Muslim girls in my class. There must be
somebody I can see in the university who
is a Muslim' but I was unable to see anyone
with a scarf or any Muslim girls. A few of my
international student friends said, 'there are
some Asian students from Pakistan on different
courses,' but obviously their timetables are
different and you don't see them. That was
surprising. *In terms of having black students, I
thought that was okay*. It didn't shock me that
much because the black students who're on
the social work course are not black students
born here. These are students who came from
Africa as children, brought up here and they
want to do social work. The majority of them
come from the care side, they've been carers
in nursing and residential homes, and they're
taking it a step further. I was the only one
from the Asian community.

An older, final year male student, Gerry, is forthright in his views.

> People say they're not racist, and most people aren't. *I* can be racist at times, *I* can be a sexist pig and I'm definitely a homophobe at times, and it comes out, and I challenge myself. But I find it funny how I'm quite often surrounded by three black people, and there's a reason for that: *I grew up in Brixton.*
>
> I've never seen any *overt* racism on the course, but it's the reliance on *stereotypes.* I think there's an element of fear and ignorance, in that some people say, 'I don't know how to talk to the black student.' That isn't necessarily bad, it's just a bridge that some people haven't crossed yet. There's an element of that in some people, 'I wouldn't know how to talk to a black man' – well, have you ever tried?

Anna, 23, details her own experience in, perhaps, a somewhat surprising tone.

> I don't know, I wasn't really surprised to see them here. I don't know, it's quite a difficult one. Obviously from talking to them again, I've made friends with a few of them. I mean they all have had their own individual experiences *and their colour doesn't mean they can't do as good a job as you and I could do.* And again, I think we're crying out for *more of those* [italics added] as well. I don't think

there's enough really, for the demands out
in society.

Another 23-year-old, Gemma, perceives the difficulties.

> There are three black people on our course
> - there were four, but one left. They're
> always sort of together, the three of them, and
> although they'll integrate sometimes they'll
> kind of sit by themselves, and everyone else'll
> stay away. I say *everyone*, meaning a few people
> - but I don't know if that's them segregating
> themselves, or that is them feeling *we* are
> segregating *them*.

> But there are certain groups of people -even
> if there are spaces on the table- who won't
> go and sit with them, because those particular
> white people don't like them.

Poppy, a 30-year-old final year student, talks of other
difficulties.

> *One thing I thought early on was that some of*
> *their understanding of the language was making*
> *it difficult for them.* I did find *that,* and that a
> couple of them are quite shy when it comes to
> working in groups, and that's something that
> I've found quite difficult. I found it difficult to
> try and involve them in the group, or to get as
> much out of them as I would if I was working
> with someone else. But then, I think in some
> ways, it's very positive because they've got

experiences of other cultures and other ways
of living that they can bring to a group. But
then, if you're in a group and someone says
something about black people, then that can
make you cringe a little bit.

A first year student, Simone, 33, stresses the importance of
working with fellow students.

The people we're going to be working with
aren't all going to be white, British, middle
class people. They're going to be people of
different cultures so I think that's something
that's lacking on this course - *an understanding
of different cultures*. I wouldn't say that I
understood all the different religions and the
things that people have to do to practice that
religion. I think sometimes assumptions are
made about them [black students]. Like in
one of the courses, the other day, someone was
just like, 'oh, we have Muslims in this class' and
everyone was looking round thinking, 'who're
the Muslims?' because [the black students]
they're Christian [laughs]!

A male final year student, Jonny, 40, views the issue somewhat
ironically.

It makes me laugh. Coming from Leeds, the
interesting thing for me is that it must be like
the 1960's. I still laugh when I walk around
here, it's almost like I'm walking on another
planet. I'm just wondering how much the

representation of minorities is also there in the
teaching staff? I go to a social work placement
and it's not there either. When we go into a
classroom, the minorities sit together. I find
that quite interesting and a little bit worrying
really, that we've got a situation where people
feel that's where they'd rather be, or where
they feel most comfortable. *I've heard racism
on the course. That wasn't about colour, but about
Polish immigrants and, you know, 'sending them all
back home.'*

Q. How do you think the black and minority
   students feel?

There's a Chinese student, she's lovely, but I
do wonder sometimes how easy she's finding
it interacting with others. There're also things
going on *within* black students, I think, about
how they perceive the situation, and we need
an open discussion about that. *Because in the
end all that's going to happen is that this is going to
produce white-middle-class-non-political-procedure-
following-social-workers.*

Betsy, 28, a final year student, ends on a more optimistic note.

I only speak to two of the black students,
really -out of the three of them- and they've
been fantastic. I was on placement with one
of them last year. She was someone who
I'd never really spoken to during breaks in
lectures, because you kind of had groups form

and the black students hung around together,
so it meant that during breaks and other times
I wouldn't see them other than to say 'hello' to.
Then being on placement in my second year with
one of the black girls -I hate calling them that, but
to save names- she was just brilliant and we're the
best of friends now.

Apolitical students

The 1970's was the decade of so-called 'radical social work.'
What this *actually* meant was the publication of 'radical' text
books which, among other things, connected the '*personal*
with the *political*,' and espoused Marxist and Feminist ideas
(see, for example, Bailey and Brake, eds. 1980). It was also the
decade in which a number of social workers attempted to
connect with trade unionism and working class movements
and focus on welfare rights work. It's fair to say that nothing
of *lasting significance* emerged from the decade: moreover,
the complex problem of trying to change the social world
-especially social and economic inequalities- while, *at the*
same time, dealing with an individual or family's *immediate*
problem, remains unresolved. Within the 1970's and indeed
the 1980's, recruitment to social work courses included both
the politically motivated and politically engaged. Was that
still the case?

When asked about his own and also his peers' *political*
consciousness or political motivation, final year student Gordon,
41, is pragmatic.

Politicians always go on about not
underestimating the general public. I actually

underestimate the general public *all the time*
- we wouldn't be in the shit we're in now if
it wasn't for the general public accepting and
believing all the bullshit we're fed. So the fact
that the majority of students are *apolitical* hasn't
surprised me at all. It's just a sign of the times
really. I'd like to shake most of them.

Marion, 41, a final year student, concurs.

I'm not entirely sure that some of them have
any political views. I've never heard anything
said by them that would give me an indication
of them having a political view.

But, you know, I don't know, because at 18,
19, 20, I probably didn't have many political
views. But then, I wasn't in social work and
my political views have increased as I've been
doing the course.

"Should social workers be political?" we asked Chris, 27, a
final year female student.

Slightly I think, just aware of changes in
society and politics and things that may
influence a person. *I think in a way you want
social workers to be a bit wishy-washy and not to
be set to a religion or set to a political party or a
way of thinking.* Because, you've got to adapt
yourself to everybody else, in a way, when
you're working. In your personal life I think
obviously it's everybody's free right. The same

for the clients as it is for us, free to do what
you want and be the way you want. But when
working, I think it's important to be open-
minded and not be set in a certain way.

Stuart, 32, forcefully expresses his opinion of both his peers
and lecturers.

This is the most non-political institution going
and it's funny - I had a conversation with
another lecturer the other day about how
I'm really frustrated. In fact, I'll go so far to
say *I am fucked off with the non-political-ness of
this place.* Social work is political -not even
social work, *education*- it's absolutely political.
But particularly for me, social work is the
most political subject you've got. You can't
be neutral: and my view is that this university
is too neutral in its approach to social work.
This is the most challenging subject you will
get and I am talking about challenging you
as a person, challenging others, challenging
perceptions and yet we sit on this fine line.
I've made my point before - classrooms are too safe.

Personality of students

In the past, students' personalities and what has come to be
known as their 'emotional intelligence' has been, however
imprecisely, monitored and measured as they progress
through social work education and training. Much of social
work, of course, has traditionally been perceived to be what

has come to be called *relational*, i.e., central to social work has been the social workers' ability to develop productive *relationships* with their clients – relationships wherein openness, trust, determination, support, courage and *change* can be successfully nurtured.

Indeed, the Task Force argues that social work "calls for a particular mix of analytical skills, insight, common sense, confidence, resilience, empathy and use of authority. Some of these attributes are difficult to test and there is mixed evidence about the exact correlation between certain qualifications and skills and being an effective social worker" (2009:17). Of course it is difficult to imagine *how* a selection panel could possibly test or evaluate a candidate's "resilience" or "empathy," and neither is it clear how this "mix" of such skills, emotional intelligence and character strengths can be developed. The Task Force adds that although it believes there are "many excellent candidates entering and completing the social work degree" (how would it know?), it asserts that "some courses (possibly under pressure from their institutions to fill places) are accepting people not suited to the degree or to social work" (2009:17). In particular, it concludes there is "acute concern that a minority of those accepted onto courses have poor skills in literacy or have difficulty in analysing and conceptualising, and that they lack the maturity, resilience or life experience that contribute to becoming a good social worker" (2009:17).

Of course people vary in the degree to which they are able to exercise 'emotional intelligence.' Goleman describes such intelligence as including, "being able to motivate oneself and persist in the face of frustrations; to control impulse and delay gratification; to regulate one's moods and keep distress from swamping the ability to think; to empathize and hope" (1996:34).

So, to what extent do the interviewees consider that their personality, character or emotional intelligence is recognised, nurtured or monitored by their tutors, lecturers and assessors? Perhaps surprisingly, there was very little interest in discussing this on the part of students.

Sarah, in her late 20's, and in her first year, is blunt and to the point.

> *I don't think any of the tutors really knows who any of us are really.* Not unless you're one of those who make a fuss, or fail, or don't turn up, or arrive in the middle of the course. *Then* they'll know who they are, but I don't think that anyone particularly talks to us, certainly I haven't found that. I wouldn't know any of the staff here particularly well. Or I don't think they'd know anything about *me*, because I suppose you -*they*- don't have the opportunity to.

> *I come and turn up at a lecture, then I go home and that's it really.* And then you write it according to what they've told you to write and that's it. It's not as I thought it would be, more sort of group-orientated than it is, but I think that if you never spoke to anyone here you could still do just as well.

As with his opinions about the apolitical nature of students, Stuart, 32, also holds strong views on this particular issue.

> *Character and personality,* that's what they should be measuring. That's what it should be about,

coupled with some of these theories. Because,
you know, without this focus on '*who we are*'
it's almost ignoring us as players in it all, it's
almost ignoring what *we* bring when we walk
into someone's house. It is ignoring what we
add to or potentially take away.

I think actually it's more about the *core person*
you bring. Now you can refine that, certainly,
and you can add to that, and you can even
fuck it up a bit, but the core aspect is what it's
all about. *When it's half past five on a Friday
afternoon and that phone rings and someone's got a
problem - does he go home? Does he not go home?*

Pauline, 24, a final year student, believes 'character' *is*
considered, albeit only slightly.

I think at the beginning, obviously, at your
interview, they're looking at your *character*
- I think *that* is the only reason I got in,
because academically I didn't have a huge
amount of experience. But I obviously did
something in the interview that they liked.
But, after three years, I think my tutor only
knows me *superficially*.

Students who shouldn't become social workers

We've seen that there've been perceptions of racism and
alleged racism on the degree, and in the previous chapter

I highlighted the conundrum of whether or not those people who use education to address and solve their *own problems* are best equipped to be effective social workers. Now, there's widespread opinion among the interviewees that their personality is no longer central to the social work educational process. This omission, of course, is exacerbated by the development of social work 'education and training' in which one-to-one evaluation by tutor-on-student has been replaced by the tick-box quasi-NVQ culture, exemplified by the decision to *reduce* the complexities of social work practice to a set of 'competences,' and other forms of reductionism.

The students were asked whether or not they believed there were students currently completing the course who, in their opinion, should not proceed to a social work career.

Bernard, 37, a final year student, puts a statistic to the question.

> How many would I say weren't suitable to go
> out and work in social work? I would say 10%.
> Definitely, if it were down to me - *go and get
> another job.* They might just do that, because
> just because you got the degree doesn't mean
> you *have* to be a social worker - you might
> end up working in Tesco's.

A third year student, Liz, in her mid-20's, also recognises the salience of the question.

> *Yes, there are some people here I think shouldn't
> become social workers.* It's not my role to decide
> that at the end of the day - you guys put

them on the course so you must have thought
they would be alright, I guess. It's when people
have their own very, very *fixed opinions* on
things and aren't prepared to give on that. I
mean, I've got *my* opinions on things, but
if someone can prove me wrong, or if my
opinion is going to hurt someone else, I am
happy to reconsider. There are other people,
I think, who seem to have come onto the
course for a specific purpose: *one person I can
think of is really quite religious, and I think that
she may have come to covert people.* There are
just certain people who just sit there and they
shout out their opinions - like, for example,
when we had the disabled kids come in, and
we had one of the lads come over to talk to us
and one of the girls on the course went, *'what's
wrong with you?'* Come on you are a third year,
and even if you aren't a social work student
you don't do that! She was really patronising
towards this kid. He was in a wheelchair, that
was the only difference.

Carol, 29, also in her final year, is surprised some students
have lasted the course.

Definitely, some shouldn't practice. I think
quite a few of them have disappeared over the
years, but I think there're still a few where I do
wonder, 'how the hell are you still here?' *In a
month's time, they're probably going to be working
as social workers.*

We've been quite a close group, there're just
some people that you just think, 'how the hell
are you going to survive in the real world as a
social worker?' There're people on this course
who I can imagine would be confronted by
someone and they'd just burst into tears. I just
think, 'God help the poor clients who've got
you as their social worker.'

Q. What have *we* done wrong?

Letting them continue.

Marianne, tells a similar story.

Several of them over the period of time
have really matured and you think, 'you're
not anything like you were three years ago.'
Others, I still think, 'if you came to my
house I'd probably shut the door in your
face' [laughs]. But that's the same with social
workers I've met on placement as well. There
are some I think, 'I wouldn't want *you* to be
my social worker.'

A first year student, Louise, 30, shares her concerns.

Some students are unkind about other people and,
you know, actively talk about other people. How
could you develop a trust for someone, to
confide in them, if they are gossiping and
things like that? But it gets to the extreme
where you think, 'well, what would happen if

someone ever confided in you?' and you know,
'if you can't uphold each other's trust, how can
you uphold service users?'

Lucy, a final year student, concurs.

There've been a few people, actually, that I wonder
how they got through the interview in the first place.
There're still people left on this course that I still
wonder about.

I think the massive thing is *communication*: if
you can't communicate with people then you
shouldn't be doing this. Because it's not just a
case of talking to someone, it's tailoring your
communication to different audiences and if
you can't do that then you shouldn't be doing
the job.

Finally, Tom, a male second year student, calculates the
numbers involved.

Ten out of thirty five, *ten easy.* I could
probably name ten people that I personally
believe shouldn't be social workers. No, bit
unfair – *are not ready at this present time to be*
social workers and yet they are going to pass.

The consensus was that many students are too young to
graduate as social workers. Although there were some
dissenting voices, the majority opinion was that clients
would prefer their social workers to have endured more life
experience, with perhaps parenting children of their own.

Of course, one of the inevitable consequences of lowering the age of entry to social work is the subsequent increase in post-qualifying education and the expectation that such graduates will not be able to perform immediately at a particular level.

Some black students believed they were subject to subtle racism on the degree. Sponsored students were soundly disliked, primarily for 'knowing it all,' and not entering into the spirit of education.

Unsurprisingly, the majority of students were essentially *apolitical*. However, and quite unusually, was the widespread belief among the students that their emotional intelligence and personalities ('core person,' 'character') were being insufficiently evaluated.

It was widely asserted that between 5 to 10 per cent of fellow students were unfit to practice as social workers, yet invariably would qualify and graduate.

Chapter Three

Modules, assignments and tutors

> I thought Sociology was completely useless. I
> failed to see the direct relation to social work.
> We did, I think, about 10 weeks of Sociology
> and 6 weeks of Safeguarding Adults and 6
> weeks of Safeguarding Children. So when
> you compare the two I would've thought
> there would have been more importance on
> Safeguarding than useless Sociology.
>
> *Amber, 29, first year student*

The Task Force asserts that the requirements governing the
content of the degree "are too loosely determined…[and]…
lack clarity and are not widely understood" (2009:18). At
present the curriculum is determined through a combination
of QAA (Quality Assurance Agency) benchmark standards

for social work, the Department of Health requirements for social work training, and the National Occupational Standards. However, the Task Force believes that the degree needs to be "delivered with greater consistency and a greater focus on linking theory to practice" (2009:18). Linking such 'theory to practice' is a process difficult to conceptualise and even more difficult to act upon: indeed, some might say that within the context of social work it is a false relationship, given the paucity of so-called social work *theory*.

The Task Force suggests that a number of areas of study or enquiry are perhaps insufficiently covered in the degree, including assessment frameworks, risk analysis, communication skills, managing conflict and hostility, and working with other professionals.

The Task Force argues for more use of research and continuing professional development so as to inform frontline practice, and argues that "social work needs to become a profession which takes responsibility for the quality of its practice. It should use the *best evidence* to determine how it can be most effective" (2009:6, italics added). The Task Force appears to assume that there is agreement as to what might constitute so-called 'best evidence.' Over the past two decades too much of what has been termed 'social work research' has been little more than an evaluation of existing policies and practices, 'research' paid for, invariably, by the very providers of the policies and practices being *evaluated*. Another tendency is that social work research focuses on the *obvious* – for example, lengthy, costly and expensive research undertaken to discover whether or not children in care ('looked after children') perform as well educationally as those not in care. Surely research isn't required to answer such a question?

There is perhaps a more central, maybe even *profound,* issue here: should scarce resources be spent on *researching*, say, the poor, or should scarce resources be spent *on the poor*? This is important: would the poor, in both the immediate and longer term, benefit more from actual cash or from research into their health, well-being or existential condition? Social work academia *relies* on such examples of human misery to undertake its research activities, but whether the activity is truly a worthwhile enterprise remains an ambiguous and contestable question.

The Department of Health's *Requirements for Social Work Training* (2002) demands that educational institutions must "demonstrate that all students undertake specific learning and assessment in the following key areas: *human growth and development, mental health and disability; assessment, planning, intervention and review; communication skills with children, adults and those with particular communication needs; law; partnership working and information sharing across professional disciplines and agencies*" (2002:2, italics added).

Jess, a 38-year-old final year student, undertaking her first academic course, assesses the academic content of the degree.

> I did Social Policy on my access course
> as a very brief module and I find it really
> interesting, but if you don't have a decent
> lecturer then you're a bit screwed. That didn't
> happen for me here, the lecturer was terrible,
> and I lost the plot completely – *and actually*
> *the essay I wrote was pretty much based on what I*
> *learnt in six weeks on my access course, not what I'd*
> *learnt here.*
>
> Sociology is very interesting, if you take it on
> a normal everyday level, but once you start
> getting into all the technical words it sort of

dumbfounds you. Again, if you get a crap
lecturer you're not going to learn very much.
*We had 12 weeks of Ethics and Values and it
was dire! It was just dire! You don't need 12, it's
almost like teaching someone to suck eggs.*

Q. We'll return a little later to specific modules. You
    wanted to say something about the degree itself?

The social work degree is probably one of
the hardest degrees anyone can do, because
you work and you also come to university.
You're bombarded with information from
different places: effectively you take on a
different job [practical placements] every
year for three years, so you have to learn the
job and produce work for that job, and then
produce stuff for university as well. And then
a dissertation on top of that - I just found
that a bit too much, and a bit pointless, really.
*I knew my answer to my dissertation before I wrote
it.* I think I'd have been much happier if I'd
done a whole literature review on domestic
violence -perpetrators of domestic violence,
which I found really interesting- and having
the time to go out and find new research
about it. *That* I could have got my teeth into.
But the dissertation is cut into bits so you
have to do so much on methodology -like
'triangulation'- and it's not really about what
you're really interested in. It's just a case of
writing something to fit these bits in.

Ben, 33, another final year student, expresses a more general point about the academic content.

> I did find it all a bit tedious, the idea of someone just *talking at you*: the idea of me sitting there, just listening, is torture. I'm not sure about the set up sometimes: the set up of 'I am at the front and we will talk,' and even with the best lecturers - 'interrupt me if you want to ask a question'- it just doesn't work. I personally enjoy the *interaction*. We did a Safeguarding Children module, which I think is a bit wishy-washy in terms of what it is asking you to do.
>
> Skills 1 is where you do 'communication skills' and you interview someone and you kind of reflect on your skills, etc,. *Well you shouldn't be here, you shouldn't even get through that door if you cannot communicate in my view. That should be picked up in your interview.* We're back to that issue - can you really teach that? Can you really teach someone to communicate, bearing in mind that most people are at least 20-years-old and are very set in the way they communicate. Can you teach it, because if you can, I can certainly tell you about a couple of people who *teach* here who could well do with attending *those* lectures [laughs]!

Ben widens the discussion.

> That says a lot about social work: social work is a little bit wishy-washy in that we

don't really know what *we are. To me there's a problem there, in that we're trying to nail down sociology and psychology to social work, and I'm not sure they're relevant.*

The research module, what a load of shit! We have got to go out and do either some sort of interviewing [qualitative] or quantitative methods. *Well, people are making it up* -and I'm not saying I blame them, because the work load is heavy and you're trying to get all this stuff done- and it just becomes a farce.

Q. So they're inventing interviewees, you mean?

Yeah, yeah.

A first year student, Suzie, 23, states what she *expected* and what she feels was actually *delivered.*

Social Policy, I thought was great. Something I'd never been interested in, never enjoyed politics at all, and a lot of it I thought was very political. But I really enjoyed it, it really opened my eyes and made me realise it was somehow relevant to social work, not directly, but it does definitely have a connection to it.

Human Growth and Development I was a bit disappointed in, because a lot of it was very psychology-based which is great if you already have a base understanding of it, and I did a psychology A-level so I feel like I did. But I wanted more practical things, *like how to talk to children of different ages*, because that's the thing where I feel I'm the weakest. *So the development of a child -although it was covered in psychology terms- in practical terms I don't feel like it was.*

Skills 1 - I thought that was a little bit like teaching your grandmother to suck eggs. I just thought, 'listening skills, facial expression, body language,' to me -perhaps because of my background and the work that I've done particularly with people with autism- I thought it was quite obvious really and I found it a little bit dull.

Suzie also discussed the various roles of the teaching staff.

We had postgraduate students as our *seminar leaders* for Social Policy: they just didn't seem to know what they were doing and they weren't all doing the same thing and there was conflicting information about what to do on the assignment. I didn't feel particularly supported by them.

Social Policy was all over the place and as I say our seminar was so bad! The seminar leader was, seriously, a poor soul, from a different country. We're social work students and we're studying social policy so we should be discussing more about it from a social work perspective and, for me, sitting there, we realised that we're just a bunch of students

> talking to each other like in a cafeteria.
> We want somebody to have more knowledge
> and say, 'yeah, it's not that way because of
> certain things,' but she didn't have a clue.

The organisational aspects of other modules also came under her scrutiny.

> The Sociology course was run partly by the
> Children and Youth Studies as well as the
> Social Work Department just like as in Social
> Policy - and I thought it was really, really,
> poorly run. They changed the lecture topics
> but didn't tell anybody, so if someone had
> done the reading beforehand it would've been
> completely useless. The postgraduate students
> running the seminars also weren't told when
> the tutors were changing topics. The module
> handbook was completely useless: there wasn't
> a single website put in there or a single journal
> as an example of things to look at.

However, she was more positive about the module on 'diversity.'

> I thought Diversity was great. I really enjoyed
> that and thought that was quite important
> with the multicultural society we live in. I
> thought it was great that it was covered,
> but the one session we had on religion, the
> Christian woman was so enthusiastic about
> Christianity she didn't get to talk about other
> religions. She didn't get to talk about Sikhism

and other minority religions that I know
nothing about.

Safeguarding Adults, I thought was fairly dull. I
thought it was very focused on elderly people
and I think there're a lot of other groups
that weren't covered. For example, domestic
violence was something that was missing from
both Safeguarding Adults and Children. It's
obviously an issue and was missing from both.

Ethics and values

I discussed with the students *specific modules* in more detail.
First to be considered was *Ethics and Values*, a module that
generated much opinion and discussion. Of course, the
values and ethics that underpin practice are, to some degree,
represented in the various codes of practice that students
become acquainted with. However, with a few exceptions
(for example, Banks, 2006, and MacKay and Woodward,
2010), there's been little substantive discussion on the actual
teaching of values and ethics on social work programmes.
James, in his final year, opens the discussion.

> *Ethics and Values.* Well, in the first lecture
> we had a whistle-stop tour of what
> philosophy was, and then a couple of the 'big'
> philosophers, and then how ethics is viewed
> and how it's changed and how it functions in
> society. Then the difference between opinion
> and values and ethics, and that was it. The rest
> of the module we had to go off and prepare

for what was supposed to be a debate on a
contentious issue – which wasn't a debate *at
all* because four of you sat together and you
had to script it and then stand up and read it.
So it wasn't a *debate* at all. I mean, you had to
take opposing sides between the four of you,
but that's as far as it went. *We made lots of formal
complaints about that course in that year. It went
on for eight or ten weeks, twelve weeks even, and
it could have been done in four.* We felt that the
Mental Health module could have benefited
from having the extra six weeks bumped onto
that instead.

Another final year student, Corrine, 28, concurs.

*I think ethics is part of social work so it shouldn't be
a separate module.* It should be a theme going
right the way through the whole course. And
I have to say it was a very woolly module. It
doesn't really have much substance.

Like James, she believes time could have been well spent
elsewhere.

Mental Health should've been longer and I
think possibly, within that, you should include
substance misuse, because it's quite a big part
in a lot of peoples' mental health difficulties.
I don't think Mental Health should only have
been a half module, it's too big an area in
both adult and childcare for it not to be given
the full length and we *all* felt it was too small

for such a complex area. *In childcare, we have
so many parents who are either misusing drugs or
alcohol but we don't have any training that tells us
about what that means or how that affects people.*
If you've never had any experience of mental
illness or you've never had any experience
of drug abuse, and you've never had it in
your placement, how are you going to know
anything about it?

Theories and methods of social work

Social work 'theory' is something of an oxymoron: academic
social work has always and will always be parasitic on other
disciplines. There's very little *inherent or unique* in what passes
for social work theory. Indeed, some believe that that very
fact is to its advantage: for example, Parton asserts that "social
work has not been seen as constituting an academic discipline
in its own right" and that in "many respects those involved
in social work education and research do not see themselves
as central members of the academy or the university sector"
(2001:170). He points to a paradox: "the marginality and
even ambiguity can give social work its major strength as it
ensures that the discipline is connected with a whole variety
of other disciplines and -crucially- with a range of other
activities and practices outside the university," but adds that
"while this constitutes social work's disciplinary strength it
can also lead to its weakness and undermining" (2001: 170).

Social work 'theory and methods' consists of a number
of ideas invariably originally developed within social theory,
psychology or psychiatry, modified and reinvented within
academic social work: task-centred work, solution-focused,

crisis intervention, existential-based interventions, cognitive behavioural therapy and psychodynamic models. They are not *socially* focused; instead they are social work methods that focus on *adapting or changing the individual, not society*.

Minnie, 25, a final year student, begins her discussion on 'theory and methods' with some more general remarks.

> I found Sociology quite wishy-washy, but then I'd done a year of a Sociology degree. It did give us a gradual transition into what uni life is like. I felt it eased us in quite gently using those particular modules at the beginning of the degree. To have Safeguarding Children and Adults in the first September, when we started, wouldn't have been appropriate.

> I personally find lectures quite difficult, sitting still for an hour, listening to someone talk to me. My brain just shuts off. But then I guess I knew that's what I was coming into, I suppose, coming to uni. I liked the more practical modules, like when we did Human Growth and Development and we were rolling around on the floor pretending to be babies and playing with playdough. I like that, and it's stuck in my head, because it was fun, to be honest. I've liked the ones where we have had people come in to talk to us, and when we've had the opportunities to interact with service users. I liked the Mental Health module very, very much, although I would quite like to have taught that one myself [because of family history].

She was particularly scathing about the social work 'theories and methods' course.

> Methods? Absolutely hated that one. I had
> trouble understanding the content because
> the book we were given [*Modern Social Work
> Theory*] by Malcolm Payne, I found really,
> really difficult. I became more and more
> behind with it: we weren't given a lesson
> on each of the social work theories, rather
> each week one of the students in each
> group had to go away and come back and
> give a presentation on it, but it was always a
> minimalist presentation on the assumption that
> everyone else had done their research, read and
> understood it. And when I didn't understand
> it, just giving me more information on top
> -in a minimalist style- wasn't going to help
> me understand. *Each week it was compounded,
> because I got given more and more theories and,
> to be honest, if you sat here now and asked me to
> name some of the theories, I could probably name
> a few but I couldn't tell you what half of them
> are, because I don't know.* I think that was an
> important module. You need theory, and you
> need that to underpin the work you do, so it's
> something I'm having to learn myself, now, as
> I practice.

Q. What about other modules?

> Modules that aren't *repetitive* are great. In the
> second year they taught entire modules that

could've been taught in about three lectures, but it got dragged out for an entire module. For example, *Ethics*. By the end of it everyone almost didn't bother to turn up. You knew it was either going to be repeated or dragged out every lesson.

The Law exam is crap and you should get rid of it. There's nowhere in the social work degree paperwork that says there's to be an *exam*. A lot of people find exams very, very hard, as I think was proved by the results. If I remember correctly, a few people failed in my year and no one got particularly high marks.

Another final year student, Emily, 27, discusses *methods*.

We had to read Malcolm Payne. *I hated reading him*. I literally rewrote all the chapters every week. I chucked all the papers away yesterday. You had to unpick each sentence and try and understand the meaning of a theory, then move on to the next one, and he explained everybody else's theories in his text. Each of us would have a method, and then every week we'd stand up and present it to the group. I question how much I've learnt because it feels like a whistle-stop tour. Quickly learn that theory, make sure you talk about it in this essay to get it in, get good marks, and go to the next one, because as soon as you hand one in, there's another one to be doing.

Emily moved on to discuss teaching methods.

> *I would have more seminar groups to discuss things.*
> I would've set homework reading, make
> sure you read stuff by the next week because
> reading just goes out the window when you've
> got assignments to write. I would also make
> all the year groups meet each other because I
> think you can learn a lot from each other.

Sociology

Sociology consists of numerous areas of study, various, often competing theoretical traditions, and also different research methodologies and priorities. Sociology has *always* been taught on UK social work courses. What precisely has been taught has varied between different institutions and at different times. Indeed, it is difficult to know what *ought* to be taught. To begin with, the students intend to practice as social workers, not sociologists. Moreover, on some social work courses sociology is not actually taught by sociologists, nor is it taught by sociologists in a *service* capacity, teaching to a specific brief. So what should be taught?

Sometimes, elements from the corpus of the so-called 'holy trinity' of sociological theorists -Marx, Durkheim and Weber- are taught. But this could as easily be American theorists such as Park, Burgess and Merton, or indeed the Italian trinity of Mosca, Michels and Pareto. Or three of the more contemporary theorists, like Giddens, Habermas, Foucault, Bauman, Elias, Mann, Alexander and Castells. More conventionally, sociology tends to be taught in an *applied manner*: the sociology of health and illness, of disability, of the family, of work and employment, of crime and deviance. This is taught through a mixture of 'theories' *and* empirical evidence.

What do social work students truly need in terms of sociology? They certainly do not need to attempt to acquire the 'sociological imagination.' Indeed, *sociology students themselves* rarely develop such a sensibility.

Sociology could be taught in one 60-minute session, not 10 weeks of one-to-two-hour sessions. What social work students require can be summed up as follows: an *empirical description* of the social class system, structural inequalities and the economic and occupational systems that ensure that a number of people have a far greater chance of becoming recipients of social work involvement than others; an appreciation that social work clients tend not to be Old Etonians, rather members of the working classes and those whom Charles Murray unhelpfully terms the 'underclass'; that the educational system reinforces the aforementioned structural inequalities; that often, the only avenue open to many of the disadvantaged is that of crime; that the police focus on the disadvantaged, and less on white collar crime, despite the rise of environmental, corporate and political crimes; that racism still exists, despite recent globalization processes and longer-term migration and integration; that the family has changed dramatically since the 1960's, as the extended family and an intact nuclear family has disappeared leaving, instead, the rise of the single parent family and the reconstituted family, in which children are raised by step-parents.

How can a social work student *truly* learn to think sociologically, especially given that it is social work they are pursuing and not sociology? Besides, many of the students who undertake social work education have already been exposed to sociology on access and other courses.

Tamara, 27, was unimpressed with Sociology, and her response to the question about it and other social science modules was typical.

> I found Sociology very, very difficult to
> understand and to grasp the concepts. I didn't
> know what Sociology was when we had our
> first lecture and when you get it explained
> to you with a cup of coffee, I thought, 'Okay,
> I understand what you're talking about, but
> I still don't understand what it is, and I'm
> not quite sure what it is I'm supposed to be
> thinking about or reading.'

Benazir was more concerned about how the module was organised and delivered.

> Sociology. We're having [sic] this lecture and
> you kind of think, 'Okay, even though we're
> students and we're not that great at reading
> beforehand,' sometimes you think, 'I'm going
> to do some little bit of reading about this
> lecture.' And you come with a little bit of an
> idea about the lecture and the lecturers aren't
> there and you think, well I spent the whole
> night reading about it, and nobody tells you
> beforehand that your lecture has been changed.
> Very disorganised. Literally, we're sitting there
> thinking we're spending this whole hour just to
> have a chit-chat with all the other students.

I believe a similar *compression* of other academic subjects is feasible. Relevant psychological insight similarly could be shortened into 60 minutes, rather than 1200: personality is the result of the interaction of genetic, social and experiential factors; nature versus nurture is a somewhat unproductive debate; it's still a mystery as to why some people tend to learn to love, while others tend to learn to hate; it's unclear why some children are resilient in the face of disadvantage, while others are less so; the loss of parental love at a young age will invariably result in negative consequences; children often copy parental behaviour.

A similar compression could be applied to Social Policy, which describes and analyses the history and structure of public and social policies aimed at protecting and assisting people from, to use William Beveridge's memorable phrase, the 'cradle to the grave'; as opposed to 1200 minutes, the narrative could be as simple and straightforward as - after the Second World War, a consensus, especially between the Liberal and Labour parties, emerged that policies of protection were to be developed for those who had sacrificed themselves for the war effort. Health, insurance, education, social security and employment were amongst the sectors involved. *Thematically*, means-testing as opposed to universality could be discussed, and, increasingly, the manner in which those people who need social policies the least, benefit the most - in other words, the unanticipated consequence of purposeful social policy.

Why would we suppose that there would *necessarily* be benefits from a surfeit of information, evidence and ideas? What is the pedagogic evidence that exposure to a series of lectures with, perhaps, some additional seminar discussion, will necessarily lead to the majority of the participants either learning from such a system or becoming interested in the subject matter in hand? This is especially salient given that social work students tend not to want to be sociologists, psychologists or policy-minded practitioners. Rather, they tend to want to offer practical help and support to vulnerable and disadvantaged individuals. Very few contemporary social work students appear to be interested in 'changing the world.'

Skills 1

One of the few Black students, Agathe, 38, wanted to raise an issue about what she saw as a generic weakness.

> We had a module on Mental Health and one of the case studies they gave us was about a black woman on a council estate. But if you look at the book list, there was nothing by black authors. *Nothing.*

The Skills 1 module has already been criticised by a number of students, indeed some of them repeatedly characterised it as 'teaching grandmothers to suck eggs.'

Pat, 39, a first year student, was also unimpressed with the module, but first she made some general comments.

> *I haven't got a lot out of seminars to be quite honest.* I don't think they've been particularly worthwhile. In a lot of the seminars we were also split with the Youth Group and they would sort of chat between themselves about whatever they wanted to, really, and you'd only find there was one or two people in the seminar who'd contribute.

> I didn't like the Introduction to Professional
> Practice [Skills 1]: you know, conversation
> skills, listening skills, that one. I just thought
> it was common sense really. If you were going
> to go into a job where you were going to talk
> to people, these are all things you should know
> *anyway* and you should have these skills before
> you start. *Everyone should have developed their
> skills by this time in their life anyway.*

Some of this teaching *does* seem somewhat absurd -'how to make a telephone call,' 'how to recognise facial expressions,' 'the psychology of body posture,' and so on. But, given this era's increasing use of non-personal means of communication, like texting, tweeting, podcasting and the almost obsessive and addictive use of social networking sites, perhaps the teaching of face-to-face skills isn't quite so misplaced?

Much depends on *who* is actually teaching, presenting the material or convening the seminars. This is a theme that Rosemary, 33, a third year student, develops.

> There is [sic] differences in who's teaching.
> I think if someone is excited about what
> they're talking about, it makes me want to
> write about it more. Like the best grade I
> got was in Safeguarding Adults. I don't even
> enjoy Safeguarding Adults, but it was the
> particular lecturer teaching me, and I thought
> her approach was really good and it made
> me learn a little bit more and I was a little bit
> more excited to write about it because *she*
> was excited. I got like, 70 something percent,
> which I have never got again and I think that

was the reason. Social Policy: I don't know
about everyone else, but I hated it and didn't
understand it. I read up on it, I asked people,
including someone who'd done a Social Policy
degree, and *he* couldn't even explain it to me.

I don't like just PowerPoint. I don't think
it's a very efficient way to teach. If it's just
PowerPoint, in my head I'm like, 'I could have
just read this at home.'

Skills 1: things like interview skills, we did a
tiny bit. *We did it in our first year and I think it
would be a bit more appropriate to do it in our last
year because a lot of social work is talking to people
and trying to get information from them - in a
nice way.* So I think it would've helped more in
our last year to just do a little bit more on the
practical skills.

Another student, Jo, 24, a third year, believed there were
simply *insufficient* modules on the degree.

The course did what it said on the tin. But I
don't think it does *enough*, that's the problem. I
think it absolutely meets all the requirements
of the General Social Care Council, it ticks
the boxes. But I always sat on the Programme
Board because I was quite vocal and to be fair
to the University, lots of stuff was changed
from that very first year, and continued to be
changed throughout the course.

Anti-oppressive practice

Anti-oppressive *theory* highlights oppression in societies and argues that it is social work's duty to remove or reduce such oppression. Dominelli asserts that "challenging inequality and transforming social relations is an integral part of anti-oppressive practice. Knowing oneself better equips an individual for undertaking this task. Self-knowledge is a central component of the repertoire of skills held by a reflective practitioner," she adds, and that, moreover, "reflexivity and social change form the bedrock upon which anti-oppressive practitioners build their interventions" (2002:9). Surely the issue is somewhat simpler? Social work degree courses should constantly monitor any signs of student prejudice?

We asked the students about this idea, both in practice and, more immediately, the modules they received on the idea at university. Douglas, 29, in his final year, believes in the importance of the teaching of anti-oppressive practice training.

> The whole kind of anti-oppressive practice, anti-discriminatory practice, has been a thing going *throughout* the three years. I think it can be a distraction at times, but I actually think that it's really important, in that most people are idiots. People don't understand the oppression that's been inherent in society for so long, and the movements that people create to try to alleviate that oppression. And, if people *don't* understand that, they need to be beaten around the head with it sometimes to make them aware of the implications of them being *a white social worker*.

Lucy, 29, however, is less impressed by the emphasis on anti-oppressive practice training.

> *Anti-discriminatory and anti-oppressive practice is*
> *taught in every single module that you do.* I think
> a lot of it is just because they [the tutors]
> want you to put that bit in your essay - they
> love that. PCS [Personal, Cultural and Social
> elements], if you got that in, you knew you'd get
> a few extra marks in your essay. It just seemed
> over the top at times, because I just think that *as*
> *a person you shouldn't discriminate against anyone.*
> If you ever did, then why are you doing social
> work? Or you probably aren't even a nice
> person. Actually, reading stuff about it confuses
> the hell out of you. If you start reading about
> it you probably think you're doing something
> wrong every minute of your life. I know that
> people have 'dodgy thoughts,' but as long as you
> keep those thoughts to yourself I can't see why
> you need to be told all the time.

Another final year student, Donna, 31, is also less than impressed by the emphasis on such training and forcefully expresses her views.

> I'd like to have a sit down conversation about
> what *empowerment* is, because I read loads on
> empowerment when I was doing learning
> disability, 'cos I wanted to try and get my head
> round this subject and how confusing it is. I
> don't think that most of the people *teaching it*
> know what it is.

Discrimination? Don't teach it, when it's mentioned, *bring it out,* because that's a greater learning experience to me. When someone says something, get them to justify it, because I think, through that, there's a bigger learning experience. It's more personal.

Theory and practice

Beth, 30, believes that the relationship between theory and practice is indeed important.

> There has to be a level of academia, there has to be evidence-based practice and all of that, and an understanding of why you are doing stuff. But again, you've got people coming in who sit and stare out of the window for the lecture and then never read anything on top of it. If you actually got people to do stuff then the reality would have much more of an impact. Because, at one point -like Bungle or Zippy off *Rainbow*- I put a zip in my mouth because I got fed up in the second year of being one of only 3 people out of 40 who ever opened their mouth. And it was mentioned, 'Hey Beth, you haven't said anything for weeks.' I have days when I can't be bothered, obviously. But I've been really frustrated at times by the lethargy that's displayed by an awful lot of people in that room, who just don't seem to have any interest in *anything*.

Whether the relationship between theory and practice flourishes depends, in part, on practice teachers, as Ricky, 26, points out.

> I could see some of it, and my practice tutor
> this year is very hot on methods and he'll
> always be trying to say, 'what theory did
> you use?' He was very good at that. *But it's*
> *very easy to separate the two and to not really*
> *understand how to apply them.* I didn't feel
> that I could apply certain methods in the day
> centre I was at because it was hard to engage
> with people as it was, never mind trying to
> understand the theory.

A first year, Sadie, 21, is less convinced.

> *I think a lot of the theory we've done so far doesn't*
> *seem to be particularly relevant to social work and*
> *I think it's hard to see how it's going to be relevant.*
> I think the problems arise when you're trying
> to teach everybody to become a generic social
> worker - that's such a wide area to cover,
> how is it possible that you can make all these
> little generic social workers? It's not going to
> work, because they need to go into it in such
> detail, and they don't. So, it's like a little basic
> bit of everything, and then you're expected
> to get the rest from your placement, and if
> you don't get the rest from your placement,
> then you're expected to do it in your first job.
> But if you've never had a placement in child
> protection, and you've only had a six-week

course in Safeguarding Children, how are you
then supposed to be equipped to work in a
child protection office?

Some bits of 'theory' appear more relevant than others,
suggests second year student, Sarah, 24.

Things like Attachment Theory, you can see
the relevance of that. But with other things, I
don't know, maybe not so much. But there are
certain things that I think, yes, I've seen that
on placement, and you can then relate one
thing to another.

A final year student, Sandra, 34, raises the idea of an
'apprenticeship route' to social work qualification.

They're having such a problem recruiting
social workers within statutory services and
even when they do recruit, they can't retain
them. So there's something dreadfully wrong
somewhere - why aren't people staying?
So what they've done is they've had this
massive drive to recruit ACMs [Assistant Care
Managers]. Basically ACMs are people who
come in and *they do a lot of social work without
the qualification*. Some do a lot of lower level
work, depending on their experience, but one
of the ladies I worked with has been there
for quite a long time and she co-works a lot
of court cases. She knows her stuff. She's 51,
she's applied for the sponsorship [secondment]
three times, and recently she was unsuccessful

again. She actually said to the manager, 'if you
don't sponsor me to do the social work degree,
I'm leaving, because I could be earning more
money doing another job and with a lot less
stress than I'm having here.'

Sandra further enthuses about the process.

I think it's a better way of doing it. Go in as
an Assistant Care Manager, you know, almost
do an *apprenticeship*. So you get to do the
work, a bit like the placements, but don't
come to university all the time. Maybe do
once a month or something, come in and do a
module. Or even choose modules that you'd
be interested in, that have *relevance* to *your*
practice. So if you're on an apprenticeship
for three years there'll be things that come up
that you think, 'actually, I need to know more
about this,' so you can buy into a module to
do that.

Q. Could you talk a little about the difficult issue of how
to relate theory to practice?

You don't need to know an awful lot about
the Health Service, but obviously we went
right back to the beginning, you know, how
it started and so on. Social Policy covered
masses about health, but you don't need to
know *any* of that, really, when you're out
in practice. *What you need to know is how to
communicate with the people you're with, what*

their issues are, who can help them. It's about
the commissioning of services and knowing
your stuff about what's available to people.
Use your initiative and find other services
that people can access, because in statutory
there're waiting lists. I think there should be
far more on working with Drug and Alcohol
Services, especially in children and families.
I know you're there to protect children, but
actually, if you don't help their parents, *their*
lives are never going to change.

A final year student, Chantelle, 28, is exasperated by some
of the academic curriculum.

We hear that fucking *-sorry!-* term
'reflection' every poxy day. Reflection is really
misconstrued by students. Sorry.

Kim, 23, in her final year, believes the 'theoretical' side of
the course is central.

I think it's really important. I mean it's like,
vital, in understanding why people behave the
way they do. Not necessarily agreeing with all
the theories, but having an understanding of
the different types, like the psychoanalytical
and -what is the other one?- sociological?

I think having up-to-date knowledge and
good research is really important and I hope
that I carry on reading about it, because then
you know where other people are at as well. I

think it's difficult, *writing* about putting theory into practice. I'm quite happy *talking* about it, and my supervisor said to me, 'you'll always pass when you're talking about it,' but when I write about it, for some reason it doesn't come out as I'd like it to.

A final year student, Jan, 42, was in no doubt that the problems of the degree were far deeper than simply the modules, or the problems of the fit between theory and practice.

I feel the course has been dumbed down. A few years ago the course had a failure rate which was really quite huge and a couple of years ago they kinda had a brutal branch look at what was going wrong and, apparently, they vetted people for voluntary work and experience a bit more before they let them onto the course. Apparently 9 people one year graduated out of a start rate of 40, but for the last couple of years, the vast majority of 35 have graduated. I am sceptical whether vetting people for a bit more experience and a bit more understanding of what social work is would have changed things so dramatically. I'd suggest that there's been a *dumbing down* in order to get people through. Something's been done to the course and the pressure's been eased, one way or another. I don't know if it's the work placements and the way the modules are set up, but some of the pressure's been taken off. Dumbing down is endemic, it's everywhere in education, so why wouldn't it be here?

Assessed work

The Task Force, in its somewhat vague and ill-defined manner, states that it is "essential" that universities and other educational institutions involved in social work education and training have "robust assessment mechanisms to ensure that only those who are suitable for practice pass their course" (2009:19). It is almost as if the Task Force has assumed that such institutions *do not* assess students and that they *deliberately* pass inappropriate or 'unfit to practice' students. Assessment processes are exceedingly difficult to create and manage, and most universities attempt to balance the many factors involved – the inherent uncertainty of assessment (why does a particular piece of work merit a mark of 40 and not 39, and why does one merit 59 and not 60?); human frailties and differences in personalities and priorities of individual markers; squabbling between internal and external markers; the 'mitigating' circumstances of individual students and the variations in the manner in which different academics respond to such explanations or excuses; the ideological differences of various academics whereby some are tempted to 'pass everyone' while others tend to be 'harder markers'; the pressures by university management to maintain students on courses for financial reasons; and the rise of so-called educational lawyers who will attempt to argue the case of a failing student.

In her discussion, Lisa, 24, a final year student, focused on the pressure she felt throughout the degree.

> The assignments [at another university] have been less hard than ours and they didn't do the Law exam and their dissertation is completely

different: they just do a 6000 word literature
review, whereas we have to go out and do an
entire research-based dissertation. I suppose
you can look at that two ways: it gives us a
lot more work on top of the pressure already
present in our third year, doing placements
and all that, but then I guess we've learned the
basic skills to go out and actually do research.

The assignments *all seem to come at once.*
You'll have all your assignments due in at the
end of semester one and then have all your
assignments due in at the end of semester
two, so I guess if you had maybe one at the
beginning, one at the middle, and one at
the end of the semester, there's time to try
and space it out a bit, 'cos otherwise you
are trying to juggle three things. And your
third year is just ridiculous with assignments.
Absolutely ridiculous.

Anna-Maria, 25, argues that different tutors mark differently,
and everyone knows that.

When different people mark the same subject,
you kinda get to think -especially when you
discuss them with other students - *well she's
got a much better mark than I have and it must've
been the person that marked it because we wrote
about the same thing.* You kind of get a feel for
how someone's going to mark it, because everyone
talks about the comments they've had back
and that sort of thing.

You did get to know who would give you
roughly *what mark* and I could probably
say who would give me what marks even
now [laughs]!

Leon, 33, final year student, was in no doubt.

There's *discrepancy in marking*, without a
shadow of a doubt. There are markers that are
seen as, for want of a better word, *better markers*.
It's quite apparent that if your work is marked
by a particular person it was almost worth 6 or
7 per cent more.

We had this module that was absolutely
pathetic in the second year *-Ethics and
Values-* which again shouldn't be a stand
alone module, but run through everything,
and people were actually complaining about
their marks when they got 60, because what
had happened was some of the marks were
so lenient that there was an *expectancy* that you
were going to get at least 60, or even more.

Jonah, a Black student, felt he was at a distinct disadvantage.

*I had a lower mark in Safeguarding Children and
so I felt I wasn't ready to work with children and
so decided not to work with them,* and decided
to go into Adult Services. We should be
marked the same way as other students. But I
think they should be aware that English is my
second language.

Ameera, a first year ethnic minority student, felt confused, from the outset.

> Some tutors want you to describe things one way, and others want you to describe things differently. It was quite confusing at the start *and because tutors marked differently, that's just not equal.* I might have said lots of positive things in my essay and just because for that particular teacher they weren't that important, you were marked down. You take that same essay to another teacher, and they say, 'no, it's quite good actually.' With the Human Growth and Development assignment, I remember I discussed my assignment with one teacher and he said to me, 'no, actually it's not *this* way, you should do it *that* way.' And when I spoke to the other tutor, he said completely the opposite and I was standing there thinking, 'right, which way do you want me to go?' I thought, that's not my area of expertise, I'm not a psychologist. I don't know which to apply because you are contradicting each other.

> You know I put *my* thoughts, *my* original thoughts into the assignment, and I want it to be equal. I noticed in lots and lots of younger students, they were like, 'that's the assignment criteria, so that's our essay plan,' and they would open a book on, say, learning difficulties, they would go to the index, find 'learning disability,' reference it, put it in their own words and then write the essay.

I was like, 'that's not right, because you're not
reading it. You come to university and you're
in full time education to read and study but
you're not actually studying.'

Q. It appears your criticism is aimed primarily at the
younger students?

*A lot of the younger students don't actually
understand how important education is.* If they're
not in university, they're working, while
mature students have their children and other
responsibilities. They all just want to get good
marks, but *I* am here to *explore more* as well.

Another first year, Mo, 24, focuses on the support students
may or may not receive for their assessed work.

I didn't think the preparation for assignments
was great, and the support for assignments
could've been improved. We did some extra
'skills lessons' that were kind of optional, but
I thought those were a total waste of time. It
was like, 'what is writing?' and it wasn't really
very helpful. Whereas, things like how to
do the *referencing* would be useful, because
there's conflicting information on how to do
the referencing: every tutor seems to mark
differently on it and it would be much easier
if they just had a standard format that every
tutor used, and for that to be explained at the
beginning of the degree.

I felt the support before the assignments was
very different in each module. Afterwards,
there wasn't as much feedback as I would
have hoped for. Everybody was marked
quite differently, everybody was picked up on
different points and because we got all three
assignments back at the same time, most of
us had done the same thing in all three essays
and perhaps in one, something was picked up,
and in another, something else was picked up,
which makes you wonder which one is right.

It's like GCSE's - they teach you to pass the
exam and I think it's the same for this. It's like
learning to drive, you learn to pass your test
and then you learn to drive. So that's the same
here, you try and pass.

Another first year student, Abigail, 28, also perceived some
inconsistencies.

They've all differed really. Sometimes you had
lots of feedback on assignments and sometimes
there've been just a few comments *or nothing
at all. So I think it depends on who marks it. And
I think the marks depend on who marks it as well.*
From what I saw, some people pick up on the
referencing, and that's a massive thing, whereas
other people aren't really that bothered about
it. People really panicked about the referencing
- unbelievable really, *more so than the content.*
This was because some of the lecturers said,
'we'll mark you down if the dots are in the

wrong place, or the page numbers aren't on there,' and things like that. So many people talk about that being a massive problem and a big worry for them. And again, they feel that their assignments are not necessarily marked fairly because some people would give higher marks or some people will deduct marks for things like the referencing or grammar.

Fay, 31, however, is more positive.

I think I've been fortunate to get feedback, *not everyone does.* I've seen other people and they've got none. It's quite disappointing when you've tried really hard and you still don't get the best grades. When you're standing next to someone who is getting 70's the whole way through and they're still complaining, and you are like, 'okay, stop complaining.'

Plagiarism is usually defined as the act of 'passing off as one's own' the ideas or writings of someone else. John, 22, and in his final year, is aware of students engaged in such activities.

I know one student who *bought* essays. Maybe others.

From the level of looking at books and articles as a general kind of –'oh, right yeah, I could take that quote out there'– doing that, that's common. I'm actually pissed off with the fact that at certain times people are doing all kinds of things really, from the subtle act of taking

> references from one book, to the other end
> where people are just ripping things off the
> Internet, and blasé about it too. It does piss
> you off because the one fear I've always had is
> – am I good enough?

One final year student, Rhiannon, 27, points to the specific role of her tutor in assignment preparation and writing.

> In the first couple of weeks I realised how
> hard it was and how much work was involved.
> I didn't know how to reference, I didn't know
> how to write essays, like I would write *I don't*
> instead of *I do not* or I would have written
> *I,* instead of the third person. So I had a lot
> to learn and I remember being in tears with
> my tutor for the whole of the first year just
> because I couldn't see myself doing it. On my
> first assignment I failed, I got 39 or something
> and I was ready to quit, but through the help
> and support of my tutor and through making
> relationships with other people on the course,
> I was able to ask for help.

Tutors

The Task Force believes that "academic staff need to keep up to date with what is happening in the field" (2009:18) both in practice and also in terms of the 'knowledge base' of social work. This is in itself a veiled and somewhat absurd criticism of such academic staff, of course, given it is likely that it will be *their work* that will contribute to the 'knowledge base.'

The Task Force reports that "strong concerns have been expressed to the Task Force about the calibre of some lecturers and tutors. These concerns touch on, in particular, their understanding of how theory is applied in practice and of the current realities of frontline social work. Educators need to share in the real challenges posed in service delivery and avoid any temptation to *criticise from the sidelines*" (2009:19, italics added). Is the Task Force suggesting that academics should not exercise criticism of such 'service delivery'? There has been a strong tradition within social work education -on the basis of either academic or political argument or research, *or both*- to criticise practice *so that* such practice might be amended or even abandoned.

The Task Force further argues that "universities should help students develop a strong appreciation of the need for continuous professional development to take into their future careers; *and of the importance of evidence, with a willingness to both use and contribute to research*" (2009:19). The Task Force here is repeating the mantra of the need to develop so-called 'evidence based' practice. What this *really means* is support for research that falls within existing paradigms: invariably, research that is in fact mere *evaluations* of practice. Moreover, what *precisely* does the Task Force mean in terms of suggesting that students 'contribute' to research? How exactly? In addition to the balancing act the average student performs -working to pay for tuition, coping with anxieties over loans and finance, dealing with personal and family matters, course requirements- *when* are such students expected to 'contribute to research'? And what kind of research should they engage in?

Over the past few decades, social work tutors paid considerable attention to their quasi-pastoral role, both monitoring and developing students' character and emotional strengths. Interestingly, social work tutors are increasingly expected to be qualified social workers *yet at the same time* there appears to be a diminution of their quasi-pastoral role. The reasons for this are quite obvious: firstly, the workload of the social work academic has substantially increased, especially by virtue of the demand that academics carry out research and raise revenue for the institutions who employ them, through obtaining local authority and other research commissions. Secondly, *social work has changed* and social workers are more gatekeepers and conduits ('sign-posters') to those who actually carry out relational and 'emotional work,' so perhaps the need for social workers to be emotionally intelligent has diminished.

Cheryl, 21, was fulsome in her praise for her own personal tutor.

> When I've had problems with my home life,
> I come and talk to him about it. I've talked
> to him once or twice about problems I've had
> with *friendships*. I think maybe we've even
> chatted about boyfriend issues. I've covered
> most things with him to be honest.

A 21 year old student, Alex, in her final year, also positively values her tutor.

> I think mostly my tutor was a great help and
> he was probably the one who stopped me
> jumping off the bridge [laughs]! I re-did the
> first assignment I'd failed, and it passed, and
> I did the next one and I actually got a mark
> for it which was higher, and it was creating
> the self-belief that I could do it. So I had the

academic support of someone in uni saying,
'you can do it, you wouldn't be on the course
if not, you can offer this, this and this,' that was
helping me here and at home.

But Nadia, 20, a first year, is more critical.

Some of the tutors intimidate you. They
make you feel that your question is not good
enough, or your understanding is poor.

Another first year student, Debra, 23, is also less impressed
with her tutor.

I don't feel like he could be bothered to be
honest, and I don't have much faith in him. I
don't really feel he is particularly supportive.
I don't really feel like there's any purpose to him
being my tutor, to be perfectly honest. If I had
an issue, I'd rather go to another tutor than him
and I feel it's slightly unfair that I have to have
him as a tutor for the next three years. It would
be nice if they moved it around a little bit.

Debra was asked about different *forms* of tutorials.

I think having a mixture of group tutorials
and one-to-one tutorials is a good idea *in
theory*. But in my last one-to-one tutorial I
didn't really feel like I had anything to talk
about. My grades were fine and I had almost
completed my ECDL [European Computer
Driving Licence]. It wasn't really a time that I

felt I needed a tutorial, but for those who had
perhaps failed an assignment and needed to
resubmit, then that would have been a good
time *for them*. But not for me, and I feel like
it was a bit of a waste of time. After about ten
minutes I felt like we were making small talk
and it was completely pointless.

Jessica, 26, a final year student, has no doubt as to the
importance of the tutor's role.

I think the general consensus with the students
is that if you've got a really good tutor, you're
well on the way to getting through things. If
you've got a tutor who's not very supportive
and too distracted to actually focus on what is
going on, then I think students feel like they're
on their own and that's quite a scary thing on
this course.

I think some of the tutors here believe in *tough
love*. And I think that's quite hard when they
go, 'actually, you can do it, go on, off you go,'
or 'what are you being silly about?' You know,
I think sometimes you need to justify the fact
that these students are feeling really low and
feeling ill-equipped to be able to do things
that they're doing and you do need to say,
'well, you are feeling that and it's justified, but,
you need to move past it.'

Annalena, a final year student in her late 30's, sees the issue
straightforwardly and more pragmatically.

> I think if you want to have a tutorial then you
> should have the option to have a tutorial, but
> you shouldn't be *made* to go to a tutorial.

Mary, 23, another final year student, found her tutor to be less than helpful.

> I've gone to my tutor a few times when
> I've been struggling, but I don't feel like I
> get much sympathy. Tutors have different
> approaches, but I've heard of good stories
> about other tutors and it makes me think
> that maybe I should go and see my tutor if I'm
> struggling.
>
> I had lots of issues with my family and that
> affected me, especially in my first year. I
> couldn't even go home because there was
> nowhere for me to live. So I was a bit stressed
> out, and I think it was affecting my work. So
> I went to see my tutor and he was like, 'well,
> maybe you should take the rest of the year off.'
> I can't remember exactly what he said, but I
> didn't feel like it was going to help me. I was
> crying a little bit, but he offered nothing. I
> didn't feel like I was getting any kind of help,
> and *I was just left feeling stupid*. Like a little girl
> who was over-reacting about something.

Many students either find modules too intellectually demanding ("too technical") or, conversely, too simple ("teaching grandmothers to suck eggs"). In particular, Sociology and Developmental Psychology [Human Growth and Development] were seen to be difficult to understand, while many students felt that in Social Policy it was unnecessary to be taught such historical detail about the welfare state.

Similarly, many students felt the teaching of communication skills (Skills 1) was too simple or self-evident. Moreover, there was a widespread belief that students should not have been admitted to the course if they had not *already* possessed such skills. A similar sentiment was expressed in relation to the teaching of anti-oppressive practice, where the *majority* of students felt that they did not need to be *taught* to be non-judgemental or non-discriminatory.

Two modules in particular were criticised: Social Work Theories and Methods and Ethics and Values; the former because the material was considered *dense*, the latter because it was felt that ethics and values were central to social work and ought to run throughout the degree, not taught as a separate module. In addition, both modules were believed to be like a 'whistle-stop tour,' all surface and no depth.

A recurrent theme throughout the majority of interviews was that there was a surfeit of the social science subjects, and insufficient coverage of both child and adult protection.

In terms of teaching skills and module organization, there was a general sense of a preference for *interaction* in the classroom, considerable criticism of seminar organization, but also a belief in that particular mode of teaching.

Unsurprisingly, there were variations in opinion about individual tutors and the efficacy of tutorial help.

Chapter Four

Practice: placements and assessors

> Lots of people were in family centres, children
> centres, and day care centres, that weren't
> meeting enough of their standards *and in no
> way prepared them for front line social work.*

> I understand sorting out placements is a
> nightmare, but I'd say three quarters of
> my colleagues weren't in the placements
> they wanted. *It's a huge problem.* It's by far
> the majority.

> *Jenny, 24, final year student.*

In 1990, the CNAA (Council for National Academic Awards)
made one of the more crucial decisions to the advantage
of social work education when it agreed that "*work-based*

learning could be fully academically accredited as part of higher education courses of study" (Parton, 2001:172, italics added). The consequence of this, of course, is that a 3-year degree is able to contain the equivalent of one academic year *in practice*, "as long as it meets the criteria for an honours degree" (Parton, 2001:172).

This change is controversial in itself: in what sense can a practical year be equivalent to an academic year? Moreover, there will invariably be inconsistencies in the provision of such practical years and almost certainly a lack of quality control.

Consider Hannah's [29, final year student] observations.

> I've heard stories from other people and I'm just glad I'm not them, because it sounds like it's been an absolute nightmare with their placements. You know, placements that haven't really given them opportunities to meet their learning needs. Placements that've had very little social work involved in them. I think one person ended up in a children's home which didn't have any children in it! Not going to learn much there is she [laughs]? All she did was watch television and play on the computer. But, personally, I've been really lucky and I had two really good placements.

Q. What about the form you hand in beforehand?

> PIMS [the Placement Information Management System]? I don't think they even look at it, do

they? That's how I felt, it seems a bit of a waste
of time really. What I identified on mine for
both years, wasn't anything like I got.

On the subject of practical placements, the Task Force
argues that the "system for educating social workers will be
strengthened by more transparent and effective regulation
and by stronger local partnerships between universities and
employers. This should give greater assurance of quality,
consistency and supply" (2009:7). Thus the Task Force
suggests that the current process is inadequate: in fact, the
provision of placements is both central to the training of
social workers and one which also strenuously exercises both
educational institutions and the agencies that provide such
placements. The Task Force's call for increased transparency
and stronger partnerships will fall on the tired and exhausted
ears of those already involved in the process.

Specifically, the Task Force suggests that the responsibility
for securing the provision of practice learning should be a
shared responsibility and the focus of "active partnerships"
between employers and educational institutions (2009:23).
Such partnerships should take responsibility for the "allocation
and audit of placement opportunities." Most significantly, the
Task Force argues that serious consideration should be given
to "reducing the minimum number of placement days to be
undertaken within the social work degree from 200 to no
less than 130…[as this would]…release more time to deliver
important elements of the curriculum which may not be
currently covered sufficiently, ensure a sharper focus on what
the placement is meant to achieve in terms of the student's
learning and development, and enable all students to have
better quality placements" (2009:24). Thus, the argument
is for fewer days in practice learning in, allegedly, "better

quality" placements, and in order for such placements to provide better learning possibilities and also to release more time for additional aspects of the academic curriculum. Frustratingly, the call for "better quality" placements is left undefined, and neither is the hitherto allegedly insufficiently covered "important elements of the curriculum".

The Task Force argues that "high quality practice placements are a vital part of how students develop the knowledge, skills and values that will allow them to work with service users, safely and effectively. They need to be actively managed so that the balance is right between teaching and learning, and between the application of theory and skills development" (2009:21). Again, it is difficult not to wonder what on earth such platitudes actually mean.

Somewhat accurately, the Task Force asserts that "concerns are universally expressed that many students are experiencing placements which do not allow them to learn what they need. Placements may, for instance, lack high quality supervision, guidance and assessment. Students are sometimes taught and assessed by non-social workers. Some are being passed who are not competent or suitable for frontline social work" (2009:20). As we will see, their perception is supported by the experiences of many of the interviewees.

Are placements sufficiently challenging?

All of the students had plenty to say on issues concerning practical learning. Final year student, Megan, 23, is no exception. She wanted to talk at length about her placements.

> In the last year I got a placement in a
> residential children's home which, I was like,

'Okay, I don't really know much about them.'
It was okay, I liked working there, but I felt like
a care worker, I didn't feel in the slightest like a
social worker. But I thought, 'it's okay, because
next year I'll get a statutory placement and
it'll make up for all the kind of standard stuff
that I'm missing out on.' Because I *did* miss
out on a lot, and my assessor was offsite and
she was very concerned and didn't know if I
was going to pass. *It was really unfair, that some*
people were getting placements where they passed
in the first month because of what they were doing
and I had to spend the whole nine months creating
situations in order to pass. It was a bit unethical.
For example, I didn't like the fact that I had
to *create a group* just so I could pass the group
section. I wouldn't have done that otherwise.

Q. But were there some positives working in that setting?

I think it's a really good opportunity working
in a residential setting because you get a
completely different perspective and I think
it's a really good foundation if you want to
work with 'looked-after kids.' In that sense,
it's really good and you can meet all the NOS
[National Occupational Standards] easily but
you have to have a supervisor who's creative
and mine just didn't care. He was a nice
enough guy but didn't care about having a
student. I had a supervision *once* the whole
year I was there. *Once!* But, like, he wasn't very
creative or enthusiastic, he didn't really teach

me *anything*. So I think if there was a different supervisor, there's loads of opportunities to work with 14+ teens and teen parents, there are loads of opportunities. I was making good relationships with them and encouraging them in different things and did a lot of direct work, so in that sense I think it was 'social-work-y', but very much *social care*.

Q. And now?

Now I'm at a voluntary agency specifically for unaccompanied asylum-seeking children. Most of them are about 15-years-old. That's what they've been 'age assessed' as, but I don't really know what their age is. But they say they're 15-years-old. Most of the ones I've been working with are from the Middle East. But there've been about 3 or 4 that I've had a lot of direct work with. They're mostly from Afghanistan and Iran: didn't speak English, or they don't at first and then they kind of learn it. So it has been very interesting, and also because of the fact that I'm a girl and I'm younger and to them I'm just like, 'oh, there's a girl talking to me.' Where they're from, they're not allowed to talk to girls, and girls are meant to be completely covered up.

Q. It sounds challenging.

I think it's completely different to normal fostering. In general fostering, there are loads of issues and problems that foster parents have, but with this kind of child, there's *extra. Like mental health. And they're dealing with so much loss.* So they have to be quite strong foster carers. I think all of them - bar one couple - had the right communication skills and can talk to professionals. But I did have a few issues with one of the couples, because they always came across as quite angry.

From the start my supervisor said, 'I don't know if we can meet your needs here.' She was very honest, which I appreciate, and she was saying I needed statutory experience. But in the end we agreed, and I stayed there and she gave me supervision every two weeks without fail, and was very honest about what I needed to improve on. I felt like she was committed to having a student, unlike the last one.

Q. Were you ever placed in risky situations while on this placement?

I did get locked in a room once, but it wasn't threatening. I think he was actually flirting with me. But I could have taken that as being threatening because he pulled a table against a chair and was like, 'you're not leaving.' But in his way that was like, 'I don't want you to finish your shift, I want you to stay.' I haven't had to deal with a lot of conflict to be honest. He came here from Afghanistan. I collected him from the airport team. I took him to a

foster home, which worked for a few months
but wasn't *really* working, mainly because of
his mental health needs which they couldn't
meet. *I phoned up his social worker and said, 'I'm
not happy with him moving to this residential home,
I work there and I know they're racist. I know
there're things they say and they're not ashamed of
saying them either,' so, I was like, 'just so you know
I have had experience of working in that home.'
But they still moved him.* So I had to pick him
up, help him pack his stuff in awful plastic bags
and then move him to this residential home.
And then I had to leave him there, and it was
that bit that I hated because he doesn't speak
English, and I had to leave him with people
he doesn't know. So I had to leave him there
knowing they're probably going to make fun
of him - in fact even when I was there they
were making fun of his name, deliberately
mis-pronouncing it.

Q. So what happened to him?

The guy who lived there was nice to him,
but the girls were horrible. One of the girls
had heard that if she made an allegation, she
could get him kicked out. So she accused
him of sexual assault -which they had to take
seriously- and he didn't understand what
was going on, and didn't know what to say, so
I don't think he really knew how to defend
himself. So, he had to move as an emergency
that day, which was horrible because they had

to pack all his stuff up in these bags because he doesn't have suitcases, and then move him to another kids' home. *Same situation*, where they had to leave him with people he didn't know. And one particular girl said to her friend in this new home, 'well, I got him kicked out by saying this, so you should do that as well.' So, the second home, the same thing happened, and now he's in his third home, but the police are now involved and all of the allegations have been withdrawn. But in my head I am like, 'why aren't they moving *the girls* out, why're they moving him out when it's obviously not him?'

I don't think that as final year students we should be given child protection jobs. I personally don't think we're prepared enough for that kind of work. Like you need really good analytical skills, really good judgement and a really good foundation of theory and practice which I don't think you have until you've worked for a little while.

Q. But some of our students will soon be working in child protection?

Yeah, nearly everyone I know who's got a job has got one in ISDA [Integrated Service Delivery], which is basically child protection. They've changed the name, because they like to change names [laughs].

James, 43, was less than happy with the placement system. He began with a discussion of both the PIMS forms and also the tutor who administers them.

> The forms are bullshit. It seems to me -nice
> bloke that he is [said sarcastically]- that the
> tutor in charge gets a list of placements,
> doesn't seem to look at what people have
> requested and just sends people out to
> wherever they sort of fit. There might be
> a whole world of intricate detail behind
> that, but there've been so many dangerous
> situations that people have been put in, there
> doesn't seem to be an awful lot of thought
> gone into it. For example, the blind student:
> she turned up on the first day to her new
> placement, and they hadn't been informed
> she was blind! They looked at her, 'what the
> fuck are we going to do?' and she had to go
> off and get another placement [laughs]!

> Personally, both my placements have been very
> interesting. I have specifically asked this year
> not to go into older persons' services of any
> description, or in a hospital placement because
> of my medical history, and I was put in a
> *hospital* with *old* people [laughs]!

Q. Really?

> *Yes*. I ticked just about every box that *wasn't*
> older people's services and I also put in the
> 'special request box' -due to the fact that

I've got no spleen so my immune system is shot, in much the same way as a person with HIV has a limited immune system- that I couldn't work in a hospital situation. *I was put in the grounds of a hospital, working with people in the hospital.*

I was put in a lot of very risky situations in my placement last year in children's services, which I enjoyed, to be quite honest. I didn't really realise at the time, not until there was enough time to look back with a bit of hindsight, but now I can appreciate some of the risky situations I was put in, as an inexperienced male worker working with a lot of vulnerable women and children.

Q. What was your supervisor like?

I was quite lucky last year as I had a very experienced practice assessor who knew the job very well, but was also snowed under with her own workload. Children's services - the whole environment they were working with had just been ripped apart, with lots of staff redundancies and people being forced to go off here and there and all the cost cutting. I walked into the middle of that and it was like walking into the middle of Beirut. But she was great, I got a lot out of it, and the learning curve was huge. I always knew that the bureaucracy was going to be one of my biggest challenges, and it was. Court reports

and all that kind of stuff. I'd never written
anything like that in my life. All I've learnt
about writing assignments has to go out of the
window when you're writing court reports
and diary notes.

Q. Can you elaborate?

You write an assignment, you've got your
own opinion, you can make stuff up and you
quote. Court reports and diary sheets must be
completely accurate – 'so and so arrived, she
was happy, no she wasn't. How do you know
she was happy? She was putting on a face.' It
was all that kind of stuff, those details that I'd
spent 3 years learning to write in one way, I
had to change it all to write it in another way.

Q. Did any of the other students complain about the
placements they were given?

A couple of people challenged the placements.
It wasn't looked upon favourably at all: but
why not? A colleague had a lot of problems
on his placement. His assessor sounded really
quite obnoxious – 'oh you can't work here,
you can't speak English properly.' 'Yeah, but I
just speak with an accent, try and understand
me,' but 'no, no, no, no.' Luckily, he managed
to work through that with some support.

I know there're people out there who have
done next to nothing for their practice assessors,

and others that've had to do an awful lot. I think I've been somewhere in the middle. *You know the National Occupational Standards? I go away and write up that I achieved this one with this person, that one with that person, and have big, big reams of paper 'evidencing' each National Occupational Standard, yet other people have just been ticked off by their assessor, 'oh yeah, you've done that.'* So that's the luck of the draw, as I see it.

The QAA [Quality Assurance Agency] *Code of Practice* states that, for 'work-based and placement learning,' the student must have "adequate/appropriate opportunities to achieve the intended learning outcomes during the work-based or placement learning" (QAA, 2007:10). It is, however, uncertain how this demand is monitored. The Department of Health's (2002) *Requirements for Social Work Training*, states that the standards for the award of the social work degree are "outcome statements that set out what a student social worker must know, understand and be able to do to be awarded the degree in social work." The document adds that the National Occupational Standards for Social Work set out what employers require social workers to be able to do on entering employment, and that these standards form the basis of the "assessment of competence in practice." Importantly, it adds that "social workers will be required to demonstrate competence across the full range of standards before being awarded the degree" and that "*practice is central to the new degree, with academic learning supporting practice, rather than the other way round*" (2002:1, italics added).

The *Requirements for Social Work Training* specifies, in somewhat incomplete detail, the basic qualities a candidate must demonstrate in order to be awarded a social work degree:

- all entrants have the capability to meet the required standards by the end of their training and that they possess appropriate personal and intellectual qualities to be social workers.

- ensure that representatives of stakeholders, particularly service users and employers, are involved in the selection process.

- ensure that the teaching of theoretical knowledge, skills and values is based on their application in practice.

- ensure that the principles of valuing diversity and equalities awareness are integral to the teaching and learning of students.

- ensure that all social work students spend *at least* 200 days gaining required experience and learning in practice settings. Each student must have experience: in *at least* two practice settings; of statutory social work tasks involving legal interventions; of providing services to *at least* two user groups (e.g., child care and mental health) (2002:2).

The National Occupational Standards for Social Work itemise 'key roles' for trainee social workers and indeed newly qualified social workers:

- Prepare for and work with individuals, families, carers, groups and communities to assess their needs and circumstances.

- Plan, carry out, review and evaluate social work practice with individuals, families, carers, groups and communities and other professionals.

- Support individuals to represent their needs, views and circumstances.

- Manage risk to individuals, families, carers, groups, communities, self and colleagues.

- Manage and be accountable, with supervision and support, for one's own social work practice within one's own organisation.

- Demonstrate professional competence in social work practice.

Lauren, 24, reiterates one of Megan's earlier points, namely, that some of these placements do not appear like conventional *social work* placements.

> *Neither of my two placements have been social work placements.* The time constraints, the lack of resources and how to deal with the time pressures – you're not taught *any* of that stuff and fundamentally that does play a really, really big role when you're out there practicing. Also, how to challenge the abusive behaviour you're going to get, that someone might get abusive and aggressive and you can do this, this and this. *Until you actually experience it, and have someone tell you to 'fuck off and die, I'm going to kill you,' you don't know how to deal with it.*

Q. Do you think that placements enable you to do that?

It depends where you're placed. Some
people's placements, from what I understand,
haven't been in brilliant settings for learning
to be a social worker, they haven't had the
right opportunities, whereas, although my
placements haven't been social work as such,
they've been in situations where I can work
around social work.

Like one of the girls on our course had her
placement with homeless people, and she'd
go in there and do puzzles with them every
day and maybe fill in a form or two. That
was kind of the extent of her placement and
although she really, really liked it there, how
does that compare to going out there and
actually doing the job?

Q. What was *your* first placement?

Well, my first placement was in the youth
offending team. I've never really worked
with teenagers so it gave me that experience,
because they were sort of 10-11 up to about
18. I think there were certain things you
can take away with you, like I've never been
sworn at so much in my life, threatened or
abused as when I worked with the youth
offending team! I still don't tolerate it,
but it doesn't faze me as much as the first
time I had a fist in my face with somebody

threatening me. That took me by complete
surprise - skills like that, I've taken back.

My second placement's a good placement for
learning my theories and that sort of stuff, but
it's a therapeutic placement. It's a mental health
service for kids and it's giving therapy. I'm not a
therapist, I've no intention of being a therapist.
And granted you have to use some techniques
-therapy kind of things- when working with
families and that sort of thing, but to me that's
not social work. They call themselves social
workers but to me that's not social work.

Eleanor, 33, a final year student, reflects on *all* her placements,
and argues that the placements are insufficiently challenging.
She addresses the question of whether or not the course
prepares a student for an actual job in social work.

I've had low points. I think some of the
placements are completely inappropriate. Like
the CAFCASS thing, it's inappropriate for a
student. It's not a learning environment a lot of
the time, because you haven't got the support
network. You know it's such a busy team that
I think you're at risk of bad practice a lot of
the time and I think you need to be a bit more
protected than that. The third year is a very
stressful time to be doing something like that.

*Some of the placements just aren't challenging
enough.* You know, I think you really have to
be *inventive* to get learning experiences out

of some of them. I think everyone should
have a local authority placement. I know it's
not always possible though, because there's
not enough support in there and there aren't
enough placements.

I've enjoyed my local authority placement
-well actually it was a private organisation
placement- and I've had a bit of experience
of how the local authority works, *but I still
feel that if I go on my first day to a local authority
job I'm not going to know anything and I'm going
to have to blag it for a good six months.* I don't
know all the forms and stuff, I wouldn't know
the computer system, I wouldn't know what
all the terminology is.

She adds a final, and interesting, point.

Placements can make or break your career in
social work. You wouldn't stay in *a job* that
didn't support you, whereas you have to stay
in your placement and that's the difficulty,
because actually when your protective instincts
and your self-knowledge would make you
walk away and try something different, you're
actually having to stay there. That can break
people, especially with the rest of the stress.

*The assessment in your placement is pretty much
like an NVQ. It's pretty standardised, you have
criteria, you've got to meet them and it just means
that you've got to 'do that' and get it ticked off.*

PIMS and the administration of placements

As we have seen, the administration of the placements, from the completion of the PIMS forms onwards, has been mentioned as being inadequate. Debbie, 24, first year student, joins the debate and expresses an all too familiar grievance.

> I thought the PIMS thing was a disappointment, because what you put down on there wasn't met – so what was the point in doing it? Just dish out placements, because that's what you're actually going to do. Just dish them out – it is just a whole load of paperwork for nothing.
>
> [Certain placements] I think, didn't appreciate the amount of work that they'd have to do if they had *two students*. And I don't think that the manager had consulted the team enough about exactly what they were going to have to do because of two students.

Emma, 25, a first year student, was similarly concerned about the PIMS forms, but also widens her discussion and critique.

> I had concerns about how much attention was going to be paid to what we put on the PIMs forms. Because, obviously there's only a limited number of placements, so it's kind of pot luck as to whether you get what you've put down, with that number of students. And with a limited number of placements, there're going to be some that're better than others.

I'm a bit confused: before, you had to do a
placement in children and a placement in
adults - *now* they're expecting you to do a
placement in voluntary and a placement
in statutory. However, if there aren't those
placements available, as long as we have two
contrasting placements then that satisfies the
course. That's my understanding of it. Which
is quite ambiguous really, because a *contrasting*
placement might also be impossible.

Q. So what's your current placement?

I'm working in a refuge for victims of
domestic abuse. There's an assessor -she's not
actually been there for the last few weeks, she's
been on leave- so I've only spent about 5
days in her presence. There's been an on-site
supervisor and she's been quite good, but I feel
like I've been quite neglected. I've had one
supervision, and that I had to push for.
But I had issues that I needed to raise with
my practice assessor and so sort of really
encouraged her to book an appointment,
but then she had a phone call that she had
to take for 40 minutes so, fair enough, my
appointment was cancelled. But I couldn't get
another one until the following week and I
was told it would be a joint supervision with
another student. At the next opportunity I told
her I didn't think it was acceptable because
that's not my understanding of supervision.
As a matter of fact, part of my issue was *with*

the other student, and I felt I couldn't speak
freely while she was there. She's a seconded
student and has a lot of knowledge, a lot more
than me. So I think I compared myself to
her a little bit too much, which I think was
part of *my* problem. But she's been incredibly
negative about my practice assessor, who has
a reputation anyway for being a bit of a bitch.
She's quite intimidating: she's quite *oppressive*,
which in the sort of environment where
you're trying to empower women sort of goes
against all of that. So when she went on leave,
a lot of the full-time members of staff basically
slagged [sic] her off. And this other student
just doesn't feel like she should put up with
the assessor. And although I think, 'yes, she is
oppressive,' the other members of staff have
also said fantastic things about her. If it was
really that awful, they'd have left by now. I just
found the other student incredibly negative,
all the time.

Q. Can you elaborate?

She'd been asked to do things that she didn't
agree with, and instead of approaching the
person who'd asked her, she stormed off and
was slamming doors and was grumpy with all
the other members of staff. This gave me the
opportunity to speak with the assessor, because
I had issues about things like the learning
agreement not being completed, because she
hadn't made time for that. I had concerns

that I wouldn't be able to do *outreach* work,
where they see women who may still be with
the perpetrator, or who may have just moved
out of the refuge or who need support in the
community. The plan -when we first went
to meet the assessors- was that we'd do half-
and-half. But I was given the impression that
-because I don't have my driving licence yet-
I felt that there was an atmosphere of them
not believing me, and a lot of the work was
directed towards the other student, because
she was already driving. So I just wanted
clarification that I'd be able to do that, which
I got. And I got an apology for not having
more supervision.

Q. So what do you actually do at the refuge?

I do whatever they need. We've helped clients
with claiming for housing benefit, which they
must have to stay in the refuge. We help them
with whatever they need and support them
with *whatever decision they make.* So if they
decide to go back home to the perpetrator
we'd support them in that. If they wanted to
be rehoused locally, or move to another refuge,
we'd support them in doing that.

Q. You said you wanted to talk about some of the other
students' placements?

*A lot of students are in settings that're nothing
to do with social work.* I think a lot of them're

worried that they're not going to meet the National Occupational Standards and it's not going to be a positive learning experience for them. *It's not actually going to help them when they're qualified.*

In an ideal world, I'd have better quality placements and perhaps divide it in the third year to be more specific about what you're doing when you're finished. I think also to have more idea of what social work jobs are available, as that's something I feel I don't know. If I had a list of the jobs that I could go into at the end, I'd have more of an idea of where to direct myself.

Q. I gather you've a very *pragmatic* view of the placements?

I'm free labour. They're a charity and they don't get any money from anybody: they don't get money from housing associations or the government. So, yes they want us there. I don't think they mind doing the practice assessing part, so I think they're fine with it. Other placements? I can only speculate that perhaps some of them are incredibly busy, and we students are a bit of a hindrance. Whereas, with mine, we can actually help them because we can work for them for free.

Another student I know works in a 14 plus team, so she has a number of different contacts and says that everywhere is fed up

with students. But then I've also spoken
to a CAFCASS officer who's a practice
assessor, and he loves having students because
-although 'they are bloody hard work'-
they come with a lot of fresh knowledge
and information.

Specific issues

Dee, 28, offers her own particular experience based on the
fact that she was a *sponsored student* and that her placement
was in the same authority she was employed by.

I can't say I've actually learnt anything on my
third year placement because I'm doing the
job I was doing before I came on the course.
The only difference is I have a different title.

Q. Do people treat you as a student or as an actual
social worker?

Not as a student. My onsite supervisor is my
actual manager. It was a little bit fluffy for me.
It was working in the Drug and Alcohol team
but working with the families and friends of
people who abuse, so not the people who are
misusing substances. So it was very much in
like a counselling role, non-directive.
I did actually say to my practice assessor in
the end, 'can I try a different way of working?'
I was thinking of one woman who'd been
coming to the service for about 9 months

when I first met her. She came every week
to sit and have the same conversation about
her life, because her husband was drinking.
And I said to my practice assessor, 'how do we
ever help this woman move on if all we do is
sit there and go, "so, what would you like to
happen?"' Well, we know what she'd like to
happen but actually the issue is what can she
do for herself? She can't do anything about her
husband, he's a drinker, he is what he is, what
about you? Let's look at you, how can we
move you on?

Michael, a Black student, recalls in detail his somewhat
negative experience of practical work. He believed that his
adverse experience was because he was an ethnic minority
student.

My first placement was at a day centre.
I think the manager of the place had *issues*,
because she didn't like me at all, although
I was doing nothing wrong. It was an
observation placement, and her job was to
observe me, work together and prepare me
for the second year. It was a day centre,
with not much going on there in terms of
real social work. The best thing to do is to
interact with the service users, play board
games, that sort of thing. Meal time, sit with
them, games and that sort of thing, *I was
doing all of that*. But she said to me that she
didn't feel I was ready to be a social worker.

Q. Had you actually asked for a placement like that?

I don't think you always get the placement
you want.

Q. What was your second placement?

I didn't expect to be in a hospital, because I
asked for Adult Services, but not a hospital.
It's hospital social work in Adult Services.
Basically we discharge people from the
hospital back into the community, with
services we think will help them cope at
home. Sometimes they don't go home: they
just go somewhere else or to respite care. I've
not had any experience of care management
and didn't have any of those skills. Eleven days
I'd been on placement and my practice assessor
was asking me to start doing interviews and
assessing people and I didn't feel I was quite
ready to do that. I wanted to look around,
learn more, get my confidence, *then* be able to
start making assessments. But I was pushed
and he said to me that he'd changed his mind,
he didn't think I was 'going to make it' and
was advising me to find a different placement.
And I said 'why?' and he said 'you're not ready,'
and he wasn't willing to work with me. I was
very, very upset about that.

The university got involved, we talked and
the university said, 'well, even though you
feel you're not ready for that, you've got to

do something about it,' so I was pushed into doing a couple of assessments. They weren't really good until towards the end of the year when I became confident. In the new year I was then very good with my assessments. My practice assessor finally became happy with my assessments and the way I was doing things and he said, 'well, now I'm confident that I can pass you, you're doing well.' But we had other social workers in the team who were still feeling negative about me.

Q. Can you elaborate?

In the beginning my practice assessor said he found it very difficult engaging with me. But now he's learnt to work with me so he doesn't think he has a problem with me and he doesn't think I'll struggle anywhere in the social work field. But we've been reflecting on why other people have negative feelings about me, and he said to me he thinks it's something to do with culture. *He thinks it's racism.*

Q. You're Black - simple as that?

Yes, and I just don't understand why these people are social workers in the first place.

[But it's not just social workers who are abusive.] I went to assess someone in the hospital, a very difficult woman. Normally, before you pass on information you'd ask

for consent to share information with other
professionals, and even if you're going to write
a care plan they need to sign paperwork. She
refused, and when I left she asked to see her
consultant and used a lot of racist language,
which they didn't want to tell me about it
because they felt it was inappropriate. It wasn't
very nice.

Jane, 32, is another first year student. Her placement
experience highlights the complex problems involved in
'matching' a student's 'knowledge-base' with the placement
experience. Jane also offers some strong opinions as to the
social work 'role.'

I think it was all left a bit 'last minute.' We could
have done with a little more time to know
where we were going, the hours of work, things
like that. We were told a week or so before,
so it was then a mad panic to try and organise
it. So with two children that need childcare, it
could've been a little better organised I think.
*We had an introduction workshop day which I think
was really a waste of time. It could've been about half
an hour.* It was again just basic things -do you
shake people's hands?- just silly things which,
by the stage that people are at, they should
know these things already. I think some of it
can be a bit patronising.

I've got a senior social worker who's my
practice assessor. It's a multidisciplinary team,
working with people of working age. So I've

been out on mental health assessments with her, seeing people who need to be sectioned. I've also shadowed psychiatric nurses and done ward rounds. So although I phoned up and arranged the days myself, *she* didn't book any of them. *So, I have got out of it what I've put into it.* And, if I hadn't been very pro-active, phoning up and asking people if I could go out with them, then I think I'd have been stuck in the office not doing a lot.

Q. What do you know of other students' experiences?

Things like day centres and stuff like that I really couldn't do that, it's just not what I want to do and I don't have any interest in doing that at all. I don't see what they're going to get from it. I spent a day at a homeless shelter, and there was one of our students there and it was, 'what can I do here?' There wasn't actually a social worker there, no one spoke any English, so I don't know how she could've spoken with the service users or anything else. *How's she going to learn anything in 100 days of making tea in a homeless shelter?*

Q. Mental illness was new to you, wasn't it?

Absolutely. I went to a custody suite where there was a young girl with schizophrenia and she was in quite a state. She'd been in a cell for quite a few hours, she was completely naked - had taken her clothes off and decided to urinate on them. She was banging

her head against the wall and pretending
to be an animal.   The social worker I was
with couldn't engage with her and nor could
the doctors because she wasn't listening. It
was quite emotional to be there and watch
it. I then saw her again on the ward some
time later. Obviously, she didn't know that
I'd seen her before, because she wouldn't
have remembered. It was nothing I'd ever
experienced before so I was, I suppose, just
really shocked at how quickly someone can
become very ill - because the week before I'd
seen her and she wasn't ill to that extent.

Q. Do you feel kind of welcomed in your placement?

*Lots of people don't welcome having students, lots of
staff there are not very keen that I'm there and it's
quite obvious that they feel I'm just wasting their
time.* Also, why should they want to help me
too much if I don't even want to work in that
field? Also, they sort of assume that you know
things and I'm not going to say, 'no, I don't,' so
I'd rather find out about it *and I do.*

Some of the social workers I've been out with
and shadowed, it's like they help clients do
shopping, go to the hairdressers or just take
them for a coffee. Well I'd have thought that
social workers would be managing the cases
that can't be managed by a support worker. *I
think that they hold very big case loads but some
of these could be given to support workers who*

don't need to be well trained and who can go for coffee and things like that. I don't think that, like, taking someone's rubbish to the dump because they can't do it, is really a social worker's job. But I think that people don't like closing cases and giving them to someone else. It seems that they like to hold on to some of these and I think that then people become a little bit too dependent – 'yes, my social worker comes round and takes me for a cup of tea once a week.'

Two conflicting placement experiences

An ethnic minority student, Rani, 22, a first year, felt her placement was inadequate. She begins her account by discussing her preliminary 25-day-placement.

The 25-day-placement was very poorly arranged. They send me [sic] in a residential care setting, with people with learning difficulties. They don't have a social work role in the placement which is fine for 25 days, because, yes, I'm experiencing working with people who have difficulties, I'm getting to know them, their needs, their day-to-day life. *But my practice assessor doesn't have any idea what I need to learn. He's a qualified social worker, but he doesn't do social work, he's a manager of a residential care home.* All he does is like – 'the money's in, the money's out, support workers are here or not, a social worker is coming for this appointment.' I can understand the thought that it'd be a good idea for me to see them in residence, but then, after three years when I'll be in a job, nobody's going to tell me how to be a social worker. They'll expect me to get on with my job, but I don't know that job, so how the hell am I going to do it?

I spoke to a social worker when he came for a review, and he said to me, 'well, the first year is all about assessment isn't it?' and I was like, 'yeah, but I haven't done any.' I can say what I've *read* about assessment, how it *could* be done, but I have no idea how to *do* the assessment. I'm in a residential home, I'm learning how to communicate, but these people communicate to me comfortably because they're seeing me every day. When I'm a social worker, they won't see me every day. So how am I going to communicate with people who I don't know, or if I have to do the assessment in an emergency? How the hell am I going to be able to do that? I'm not the only one.

Q. What do you mean?

First of all we had Min [a fellow student] who lives with me and she was sent to a child protection team. The practice assessor didn't bother to tell the university, 'well, actually, I'm about to leave my job in about a week.' So Min went there for 5 days with, like, 'what am I going to do for the next 20 days, who am

I going to shadow?' *She has a struggle finding
anything to do.* She contacted the practice
assessor and the co-ordinator and they said,
'well, we'll find another placement for you.
You go there and make sure you dress smart.'
And we were like, 'what is *that* supposed to
mean?' We're not children!

It is disorganised everywhere. When I worked
in residential care there was one person with
MRSA and they didn't tell anybody about
it. You're meant to tell the support workers,
you're meant to tell *everybody* that the person
has MRSA. One of the assistant managers
didn't tell anybody because she thought people
would start panicking and refuse to work, and
they'd be short staffed. Two weeks later, one of
the assistant managers was doing the handover
and she was like, 'by the way, Charlie's really,
really ill, and he's been diagnosed with MRSA,
so be careful. I've put out all the gels and the
anti-bacterial stuff, so take it with you,' and she
was giving us the instructions and I was like,
'two weeks ago I was eating with him. So who
am I going to sue - the county?' And then
all of the staff just went all crazy, 'how could
you not tell us, you know it's very hard for us,
we're support workers, we're not main carers
or working as a nursing home, so we cannot
deal with him because he needs one-to-one
care because he's throwing up after every 5
minutes, and then we have 5 other people to
work with, how are we going to deal with it?'

Sonia, 24, a final year student paints a full and rather more *positive* picture of her experience on placement.

> My first placement was in a day centre for older people. There was a level-two social worker there who had a poor placement, as there was nothing there to meet her standards [NOS's], and she was struggling. I didn't feel like *I* had learnt anything to be honest. I only did 10 days.
>
> Level-two was working with single homeless people. Day-to-day work, and some of the things were just very basic. Getting the money off people, making them lunch and stuff. A lot of the time it was just being there for when they wanted to talk, and sometimes it would be just sitting in silence with them, waiting for them to just feel comfortable or awake enough. *It opened my eyes to many, many different issues and life experiences of people.* There were a few aspects to it that did feel at times that I was at risk. They had no cameras, it was open, people had loads of coats and pockets, they could have had knives. We had a needle exchange and I had needle exchange training, but obviously we were giving needles to clients and then they were in the building and, you know, God knows what could happen.

Q. You say you were "at risk." Can you elaborate?

I assisted a client who slit his wrists and who
had Hep C. I also had a death threat. The
police suggested I didn't chase it up, because
she was always in and out, and she was a
very poorly woman who was going to die
soon anyway. But I still absolutely loved the
placement. *My practice supervisor was really good.*
She was really confident and taught me a lot. I
aspired to be a bit like her, she was very forward
with the people - they embraced her and were open
with her. But she also maintained a very professional
role, because it was easy in that kind of setting to
just seem more like friends. But it was a really
good place to learn a lot more about people
and spend actual time with clients. We literally
had 8 hours a day to just sit with clients, no
official-type paperwork at the end of the day:
we just wrote, 'so and so was alright today,
refused to eat their lunch but was quite awake.'

I also had an outside assessor. I was really
cautious about her from the beginning,
because when she came to the university for
the initial chat she was saying, 'I had some
time out because my husband died,' and then
her cat died and then everything else died and
she was just like really emotionally unstable. I
was like, 'are you sure you want to come back?'
The things I was telling her in supervision
were just blowing her away, and I felt that I
almost had to filter what I was telling her most
of the time. Then it came to an observation
where this client -the one who, incidentally,

had later cut his wrists- was pleading with me, crying with me, and I was trying to fill out our basic forms and my supervisor actually said, 'I'm sorry, I have to go.' It upset her too much. I was like, 'you're here to supervise me. That's fine, you go home.'

Q. And what about your recent placement?

I worked with older people in a hospital, people with mental health problems and I was very intimidated by the statutory bureaucratic stuff -especially being dyslexic- writing reports and sitting in an office. Compared to last year, it was a huge, huge, difference. I'd worked in mental health before. My assessor took me round -you know, you do the initial meet before the placement- he took me round the ward, and when we came out he said, 'oh yeah, I think you can do this.' I said, 'sorry?' He said, 'well, this was the tester, this was to see how you'd cope in there.' Because it can be a very intimidating environment with people screaming and running about and grabbing at you as you walk past. But it didn't faze me, so he said, 'yes,' I could go there. It was quite worrying because if he'd said 'no,' it would've been quite difficult to get another placement.

My supervisor's the best social worker I've ever met. All the social workers that I've met go to him when they've an issue or a problem. He's been working for 28 years, he reads about law and policy in his lunch break [laughs]. He lives and breathes social work, he's such a great person to learn from. He's very accepting of me, very accepting of me being younger, possibly one of the only staff who doesn't patronise me.

Q. Can you talk about your clients, maybe one in particular?

> *Well, an older person, who'd been losing her hair.* She went to the doctor and said, 'look I'm losing my hair.' 'Oh, you are really down, we'll give you some antidepressants.' She said, 'no, I need some help. I'm getting really depressed but this is, you know, it's affecting my self-confidence, I don't want to leave the house' So she comes into hospital because she's so depressed, she's not eating, she's not left the house. The antidepressants *do* lift her mood, so she's able to eat, and I talked with her almost every other day about the benefits of eating and drinking, and trying to talk to her friends and family as much as possible. They sent her to a dermatologist from the hospital and her hair grew back and she's fine. She's back in the community doing really well for herself, and you just think, 'why does nobody pick up on these essential things in life?'

Q. What do you want to do when you finish the degree?

I don't want to sit in an office all day. I can
see why it's important and I can see that
the procedures are 'how you can get people
help, and how you can protect yourself, and
how you can use the law, and how you are
following procedures, and you're safeguarding
others.' I can see the benefits, I'm not
ignoring them. *But I want to do work where I
can spend time with clients.* You know, I visited
the Crisis Team a few weeks ago and they
said they write things on a note pad and they
spend an hour or two, everyday, with each
client for six weeks and then they're gone.
And they want to see an improvement within
a week. *That* is the kind of work I want
to do. *I want to work with people and make a
difference. I don't want to be seeing them every three
weeks for a year and just about get them the service
that they don't even want because by then they've
changed their mind.* All the things that we're
trying to give them -time, respect, empathy,
understanding- they kind of get pushed
backwards because you're in such a rush to fill
in the right paperwork and make sure you get
them the service that you can afford to give
them, *not what they really need.*

A detailed history

Finally, Abigail, in her third and final year, provides an
exceptionally detailed account of her placement history.

PIMs. What a waste of time. In my first year I
filled it all out, and obviously my biggest issue
was my childcare and having to be there at
certain times for my children. I actually put
'everything,' because I didn't mind *where* I went.
But I made stipulations about childcare and
then was really, really fed up, that I was going [a
long distance]. Obviously trying to get my kids
to the childminder and get to the placement
by 9am, was pushing it a little bit. I was even
more furious when I rang to discuss it with
the placement co-ordinator who told me that
people with disabilities have first priority. Well,
we get it rammed down our throats all the time
about 'equal opportunities,' and how everyone
should be treated the same, and I know there're
some issues with travelling and that type of
thing, but I still felt that as a mature student
with children I too should have been a priority.

Q. Tell me about your first short placement.

We did 8 days and I did one day every week
for eight weeks. I went to a child protection
team and it was *purely observation*, but I ended
up doing a load of stuff I probably shouldn't
have done [laughs]. I remember one day they
said to me there was a child who'd been found
by the police because he'd left home alone and
was actually in the police station next door to
the social services department. 'Would I go and
collect the little boy and bring him back to the
office?' Bearing in mind the staffing levels were

ridiculous there, I said, 'well, am I allowed to do
that, because I'm only observing?' They said, 'oh
no, that's fine, just nip over there and get him.' I
had my student ID and that was it. I went over
there and walked in, and there was this little boy
sat with the police officer and two other sort of
liaison officers. I couldn't work out if it was a
boy or girl because *it* actually looked like a girl.
When I first went in they didn't ask me for any
identification, they just said, 'oh yeah, just come
through.' Then I was given this little boy. They
said to me, 'can you try and find out what sex it
is?' I'm like, 'this is a three-and-a-half year old
child.' 'Well', I'm thinking, 'the only way is to
take him to the toilet, and I'll see which cubicle
he wants to go into' [laughs].

Q. And?

I take him back to the office, and they say, 'can
you look after him for a little while?' so I say,
'yes, that's fine.' So I went off into this room
and I suddenly thought, obviously, with the
things we talked about – 'best evidence' and
not probing the child, not questioning the
child– so I just played with him. And actually
he divulged a whole wealth of information
just by looking through magazines and talking
about his favourite foods and that type of thing.
And then he told me he had a brother. I'd
worked out he was a boy by this point because
he'd asked to go to the gents' toilets. I went off
and said, 'he's got a brother' and they found the

school that his brother was at. So then they said
to me, would I go to the school and 'pick up
his brother?' There was no one else to do this,
so I said, 'yeah alright then, have you got some
car seats?' So, I found this school, and I had this
other child with me. I walked into the school
and they said, 'oh, you've come to collect so
and so' and I said, 'yeah, would you like to see
some identification?' She said 'no, no that's not
a problem' and I went 'no!' I said, 'I've been to
the police station and they haven't asked me for
anything, I've come here to take another child,
I *want* to leave my details!' So they were like,
'alright, okay.' So I gave them all my details and
then took this child back. It was bizarre. I took
them to the computer, put *CBeebies* on.

Q. What happened then?

When I went to leave the little three-and-a-
half-year-old boy he burst into tears saying,
'you can't leave me' and I actually was quite
upset. I drove home feeling, 'how could
somebody just leave their child like that?'
That would be like leaving my daughter when
she was three, just with her lunch box, until
'mummy got back.' It just seems surreal. But
it was more the impact *he* had on me. I did
talk to them about it and they said, 'well, you
should have had some debriefing,' and then
obviously I got a bit into trouble because I
shouldn't have done any of it in the first place.
I think they let me do it *because I've got children*.

If I was a bloke, I don't reckon they would have asked me to do it.

Q. Ok. What about your first lengthy placement?

I was at a homeless hostel, for clients aged 18 plus. To me, social work isn't what statutory work is, you know, sitting at a computer. *This was real social work, this was one-to-one working with people*, and we used something very similar to *solution-focused therapy.* When you first read about it you think it's all a bit airy-fairy, but actually with 18 plus people who've lost their way in life, or certain things've happened to them, they just need someone to listen to them, and just by rambling on for an hour with you they come up with their own solutions to problems. They just need a bit of help and guidance on how to get hold of those things. *I think it was probably the best social work I will ever do.*

Q. And the placement you're finishing now?

I've been placed in an ISDA which is an intensive family support team, which is child protection basically. You've got two ISDA's in the area I worked in. The first team was the assessment team, and any work from the assessment team that obviously went to Section 47 [of the *Children Act*] came over to us. Then we did the *long term work* with them. So it's a statutory placement, which I haven't

done before. It's vastly different to working in
the voluntary sector. *You spend an awful lot of
time at the computer.*

Q. And how did you find the IT there?

The computer system they've got in place
has obviously superseded all their previous
paperwork. So if you went out to people
you'd fill out sheets: but the minute you do,
say you open a Section 47, you've got children
on the child protection plan, and that will
kick off about twelve other tasks. You'll
have timescales for all of those tasks: like I've
got 35 days to carry out a core assessment.
Otherwise, management are just going, 'how
many red tiles have you got?' because having
red tiles is a bad thing.

Q. Can you explain what a 'red tile' is, for any readers
unaware of what you mean?

If you go beyond the set timescales -like
35 days for a core assessment, or 7 days for
an initial assessment- you'll have a red tile
on the screen, sort of glaring at you, to tell
you that you're *out of timescale*, and obviously
management don't like that because it's not
good for their figures. And you've got *grey tiles*
and *green tiles* to show how you're progressing
with things. I think people get a bit freaked
out by these tiles. Senior practitioners that've
been there for a very long time actually

couldn't care less, and really don't care how many red tiles they've got, because they're doing the job the way *they* want to do the job. Which is probably right. *You know, families and people don't work to 35-day timescales.* I think sometimes when you write core assessments, which are quite an in-depth reports about the extended family, you'll write them but things will change so much within the timescale that what you've actually written by the end is probably *defunct.*

Q. What was the team like when you arrived?

The team itself is falling to pieces because no one wants to work there, they're all overworked. There's just too much work and not enough people. Quite a few of them are burnt out now. They've recruited two: one lady who hasn't ever done any statutory social work, and the other guy has been working in the private sector. *He* works to rule, and *she* bursts into tears every two minutes because she can't cope with it [laughs]! Everyone is leaving, so now they're trying to recruit newly qualifieds, and it's quite scary to think that they're going to have only one senior practitioner in that team. Everyone else will have no or just a minimum amount of experience. *Most of its court work, and the degree course doesn't prepare you for that.*

Q. Does that include you?

The only thing I know about court papers is what I've seen other people complete, and bits that you do on the electronic recording system which go towards such court documents. But there are loopholes in that system: you have to fill out certain documents on ERIC [Electronic Recording of Information for Children], but the court or the solicitors don't like that format, so you have to put it all again in a WORD document for them, which is crazy. And obviously I've never done any court work because as a student you're not allowed to do any of that type of work. You can be involved in writing reports but they have to be overseen, and obviously the senior practitioner would have to be subpoenaed, etc.

I've read some pretty poor reports while I've been on placement in my third year – statements that some social workers have made on core assessment work. There was one thing about, 'oh, and he was found hanged,' and that was it! No mention of who he was, where he came from. People do tend to have to play a lot of 'catch up' on other people's reporting because they haven't put down enough information. I think one of the biggest skills is writing quite *concisely* but getting everything you need in there, and there are some people who don't do that. I think some documents that've been sent off have had to be looked at by all professionals involved with that family. Some reports are quite laboured: you're not

allowed to write the word 'attachment,' for
example. You're not allowed to put anything
in like that. That's not down to you, that's
down to an *expert* to talk about. You can skirt
round the issue of what you observed, and
some people go into an awful lot of detail
and a lot of other professionals don't like that,
because you're not getting to the point. And
I think sometimes a lot of social workers
who are subpoenaed to appear in court are
questioned an awful lot because they have
maybe *implied* certain things through their
writing. So, you've got to be able to back
yourself up. So why not write it that way in
the first place and keep it quite to the point?

Q. What kind of one-to-one work have you done?

In the 18+ homeless hostel there were a lot of
substance misuse issues, and I did one-to-one
key working with people. It was a difficult
situation for some of them: they've been
dependent on some type of substance and
possibly also suffer from mental health issues.
I think some people weren't ready. I saw the
same people come back and back and it was
quite disheartening: you'd spent some time
with them, you know, you'd maybe got them
into voluntary work, things were looking
good and then the minute they see their mates
again they're coerced back into having a drink.
There's a *certain time* for some people and it
just wasn't their time. Very gracious people,

you know. I've seen them out   -because they
live in my local area- they always say, 'hello,'
even if they're back on the street. I would
never treat them any differently to how I
treated a fellow professional.

Q. Can you talk about one client, one case?

Let me tell you about a 'looked after' child.
She was 14 at the time [2009], living with her
dad who had actually taken on the children
from 2000 because there were domestic violence
issues between him and his wife. She couldn't
cope, social workers got involved, she said they
were round every two minutes, drove her mad
and in the end, she just went, 'do you know
what, you can tell him he can have them.' So
he took custody of the children and has a
supervision order on them. He's not a great
parent. He's not had a great life himself, never
worked, really wasn't that interested in his kids.
They've done exactly as they pleased, they've
had no boundaries. So, this girl, she got to 14
and he hit her, so she just left. She was placed
in the 'looked after children's team.' She was
actually just removed and put in foster care,
which actually wasn't the right thing to do,
because she was coming up for 15, and actually
someone should have been looking at the
extended family for her. Nobody did, they just
removed her: firstly, as a temporary measure, but
then applied for a longer term placement. But
when I got involved she was still 'looked after.'

I had identified members of her family. She
was very close to her mum and spent a lot of
time seeing her. So I did an assessment on her
mum and, you know, managed to get them
back living together. She had no housing,
because her mum lived above a pub where she
worked. So we had to find her some housing
that she could afford. It took a while and it
was very frustrating for this 15-year-old. She
told me to 'fuck off' quite a few times because
'I was rubbish, I wasn't doing anything.'
She was actually removed to another foster
placement. She was in a private foster
placement *originally* and because of the funding
-they wouldn't fund it- we had to put her in
a statutory placement, which was awful, she
hated it. The woman was terrible.

Q. Can you elaborate?

The National Fostering Agency which we use is
a private fostering agency, and they get paid *vast*
amounts of money for taking on children. The
family that she lived with had children, they ran
their own business, they had a beautiful home.
They sort of treated this girl in the lap of luxury,
really, compared to what she'd been used to. She
was bought a whole new wardrobe. Anything
she wanted, she got. The funding ran out, so we
had to look for an in-house placement within
the county, and they obviously have foster carers
that they pay. And it's hit and miss, so this young
girl went to this woman.

Q. The woman who was "terrible"?

> Yes. She hated this woman. I met her and I just
> thought, 'well no wonder.' I was desperate to
> get this child out of there. So I spent a lot of
> time with mum, got all the housing sorted out,
> got a property, and then moved her back with
> mum. Her other son actually left his dad as
> well and so he's moved in too. Do you know
> what the nicest thing was? I went to visit this
> child when she was living with mum. I went
> in and I said, 'oh, everything seems to be going
> okay, so I'm not going to stop too long.' This
> child then gave me a card saying, 'thank you,'
> for my help. I said 'oh, thanks very much'
> bearing in mind the last time she had seen me
> she told me to 'f off.' I said 'right, I'm going
> now then, because everything seems fine. I'll
> come back in a couple of weeks.' She said to
> me, 'I can't believe you're going, every time
> you come and see me, two minutes and then
> you're gone,' and I said, 'normally you tell me
> to get lost - are you asking me to stay?' She
> said, 'well it would be nice,' so I said, 'make
> me a cup of tea and I'll stay.' You know it was
> lovely. She would've quite happily had me as
> her social worker for life I think.

Q. Tell me about the woman who was so "terrible."

> The foster carer I didn't like was quite *loud*.
> She lives in this tiny little house, which I didn't
> think was conducive to taking in teenagers.

She'd got so many issues herself. For example,
on my first visit, she told me all about domestic
violence, her son having witnessed it and being
in counselling. Everything was about *herself*
and this woman was a bit nuts, really. She
seemed very loud and then I sort of hit on
the idea that actually the child I was working
with had an ear problem and it turned out that
this foster carer was herself hard of hearing.
So there was all this shouting that they were
doing at each other [laughs]. And the woman
was saying, 'she just shouts at me.' And I just
thought, 'it is just something to do with both
your hearing,' so we had a discussion about
that. But they just never got on. The woman
was well known within our office. They asked
me to fill out a form about how she did as
a foster carer. I put all my concerns down,
and she's just been passed to do long term
fostering! She was only respite fostering before.
It's outrageous, absolutely outrageous!

The student responses to the various questions about their
practical placements are full and comprehensive. What
emerges includes the following:

- There was disquiet over the administration of
  placements, especially the way in which student
  requests -e.g., type and location of placement, and
  relevant student familial needs- were not always met.

- Specific tutors in charge of the PIMs processes were
  roundly criticised.

- Many of the placements were perceived *not* to be social work opportunities but, rather, social *care* settings where the student would *only* learn about a specific client group, but little else. Indeed, these kinds of placements were consciously or otherwise perceived to be akin to 'free labour.'

- The student perception of *actual* social work varied, although there appeared to be a consensus that *statutory* social work was not necessarily the best place to practice what they considered to be 'real' social work.

There is absolutely no question that the organisation and administration of practical placements is the most complex and demanding social work tutorial duty, and similarly there is no doubt that it is this work-placed learning that is most significant to the degree. Reducing the days involved, which is the Task Force's recommendation, *may* make the task easier. However, it may not be the appropriate decision and, besides, it is not simply a question of the number of days spent in placement: it is the *quality* of the placement and the opportunities available for learning, the quality of the supervision involved and, most importantly, it is essential that social work students consistently and transparently receive social work placements and not only in allied settings like social *care*.

Chapter Five

Reflections on being a student

One of my reasons for doing this is because I don't want to do what I was doing anymore. I want to have bank holidays and weekends off and I'd like to get a pension. *I'm not here to change the world.* I don't think I've got as much out of the course as I hoped I would. Like the first skills module, the interviewing skills module - you get taught a lot about stance, body movements and all that, eye contact, how important all that is. I've gone away and done a taped interview. I can now judge people by their body movements, *but I always could.*

I was hoping that I'd become a better person and I feel a little disappointed by that.

Geoff, 38, final year student.

Students were asked to reflect more *generally* on the degree, and to consider what they believed its strengths were and what had disappointed them. Had the course lived up to their expectations? Was the curriculum sufficiently balanced between academic modules and practical placements? Was the degree intellectually challenging and demanding, or not? Did the course prepare them for a social work job after graduation?

Katie, in her early 20's, found that the degree was not sufficiently practical.

> *I thought the course would be more relevant to practice.* I shadowed a child protection social worker yesterday which was fantastic and I was looking at all the paperwork and everything that they do and I realised I really didn't know *anything* about it. I probably learnt more from her yesterday than I did from most of the Safeguarding Children module, which is a little bit worrying. I don't think things like the practical aspects of social work are really covered: things like the reports I'll be dealing with, because there's such a massive amount of paperwork in social work. Although it's good that we're writing essays and we'll have a level of academia that means that we should be able to write these reports, the actual practical aspect of what's involved in these reports is ignored.

Q. Do you think the assumption is that you'll learn all that on practice?

I think so, and I think that's a wrong assumption to make because a number of placements aren't going to be in a social work setting. Mine's a voluntary setting, and there're no social workers there. *It's not social work,* although I can cover my National Occupational Standards and I'm happy with what I'm going to learn from there.

Katie makes a crucial observation.

I think some people have a natural ability to be a social worker. I think you do have to be a certain *type of person* and I think maybe that *that* should be more closely monitored.

I would say a *willingness to learn* is really important, particularly with the amount of training that's involved with social work -practical training, not necessarily theoretical- you know, practical on-the-job training. Someone who can show empathy, someone who can listen and empower people and have the confidence to do so. And although I think the course should build the confidence of some people, I worry with some that it won't. Just from what I've already seen on my placement they need someone to be strong and confident and so I can already think of people on the course who wouldn't last five minutes there.

Katie also raises the issue of student finance.

I think it's forgotten that *we are paying for this*
and we should be getting a service and I think
a number of other students forget this. They
don't think that it's okay to complain about
things. So, like the issue with the placement
tutor, instead of standing up and saying, 'actually,
this isn't acceptable and I am essentially paying
your wages, you're here to provide me with
a service and that's not being done,' they say
nothing. I think it's easy to forget the actual
value that this course is. Nearly £10,000 or
so in fees [for 3 years at pre-2012 levels], and
also a maintenance loan. Having the NHS
bursary is the only thing that keeps me afloat,
and without that I don't know how I'd survive.
I do agency work, so I take on work as and
when, which works well with this course. *But
it does mean I have a lot of debt.* But I chose to
give myself less stress. So the more loan I take
the less I have to work and the more I can
concentrate on the course and placements.

Another first year student, Suzie, in her early 30's, reiterates
the point about the degree being insufficiently practical.

I thought the whole course would be more
based on *real things that have happened.* I think
it's very useful when someone talks about a
case that they've been involved with. You know,
maybe more explaining what's happened and
then relating theories to that. That would've
been far more useful than the way that it's
taught at the moment. *There's nowhere near*

enough training on this course in Child Protection.
I can't see how anyone can leave it feeling
comfortable to be able to go into a situation
like that because what have we learnt so far?
*I don't feel that we've learnt anything that we don't
already know.*

Q. What do you think there's too much of?

a) Anti-oppressive Practice [groans], b)
Diversity, and c) shadowing people. I've found
it quite difficult working with alcohol abuse,
because many clients are generally under the
influence of alcohol. I worked in a centre and
I didn't feel able to tell them to 'back down,'
whereas I suppose with more experience
I'd be able to. And I keep saying 'I'm just a
student' to people, which I shouldn't do either.

*I think the course could have been condensed down
to maybe 18 months* if we'd done it full time and
not had four months off in the summer and
a month and a half off at Christmas. I think
more people would do the course then, you
know, because it's a big financial commitment
not to work for three years. *I would've done it
a long time ago if it was a shorter course.*

Q. How difficult is the academic side of the course?

*I think it's quite easy to read around the subject.
I think to obtain a pass you wouldn't have to do
a great deal of reading.* I think if you read the

right things -you know a few pages from this
and a few pages from that- and also the fact
that so much is online. I really don't think
that it'd take a great deal of time if all you did
was online reading. But I don't think you'd
learn enough to be confident to practice
without reading the key subjects.

Mental health isn't covered anywhere near enough.
I've gone into a placement and I didn't know
what psychosis was - obviously I had a
rough idea, but I didn't know any more than
Joe Bloggs does. So I've done an awful lot
of reading up on different illnesses -separate
to anything that I've got assignments on-
because otherwise, how do I know what the
symptoms of bi-polar are, or anything else? So
far, there hasn't been anything on the course
which has actually gone over what all the
mental illnesses are. You just look a bit stupid.
It's been assumed that I know what these
things are, or what medication they're taking -
well again, I don't know that, but I started by
reading people's notes and you pick things up.
Lots of people just wouldn't do that.

Heidi, 22, in her final year, found it all too easy.

In the first year, the first thing I liked was
that *I had plenty of spare time.* Monday to
Wednesday at university then Wednesday
afternoon to Sunday *I am free* doing nothing,
just messing about, that sort of thing.

Perhaps such a candid confession adds weight to the earlier expressed view that the degree could be shorter in length, reduced from 3 years to 18 months?

Becky, 24, another final year student, also found the course far too easy.

> I expected the course to be a lot harder and I was quite happy after the first half of my first year. I thought, 'actually, it's not difficult.'

> I think most people have *developed as people*, they've learnt who they are, and they've learnt what their strengths and weaknesses are and know how to deal with those. They may be having problems in their home life but they're not the sort of problems that are going to massively effect how they work.

Not every one agreed that the course was easy. Consider Sandra's opinion.

> The lows would be, I think, *the pressure.* I think sometimes we have so many assessments and the deadlines are so close together: so, I just think the workload and the pressure surrounding it, was my low. But then you know, I have a young child -a lot of students don't- and there're things externally that I have to bear in mind as well.

Of course no educational provider can iron out or balance some inherent differences between students. Some students have major family responsibilities in addition to their learning, others are financially dependent on part-time work. Indeed, many social work students work in residential care homes and other institutions, and some work night shift or other unsocial hours.

Two final year students, however, could only look to the positive. Firstly, Kim, 31.

> It's a good career for me. I'll be staying in local authority work for a while. I like the fact that it's fairly well paid and the fact you can work your way up, I like that. *There're clear set career steps that you take.* I like the fact that I can have more training and that I get a pension and that's what's important to me, to be able to move on and progress and to have a bit of structure.

Lisa, a sponsored student, summarises her 3 years.

> Without the course I don't think I'd have worried about the theories behind the work, although that doesn't mean I wouldn't have done the job well: but I don't think my understanding would've been as great. I could've still have looked after families, I could've still helped families, I could've still moved families on, could've still worked with children, but I wouldn't have had the same depth of knowledge about 'attachment' and those kind of theories.

Q. And how does that make you a better social worker?

> I think you're too blinkered otherwise.
> You need to be able to look outside of this
> small box that you were first in to see how
> environmental factors impact - poverty, class,
> neighbourhood, families, relationships. If you
> weren't spending time considering *those* factors
> your picture would be too narrow, so I think
> what the course does is *broaden* the perspective
> you have of life. Then because you have a
> broader view, you can narrow it down in the
> right way.

Lara, a 23 year old final year student, pointed to the difficulty
of balancing home and work life.

> When I was 18 I realised I didn't want to do
> what I would call *hard core social work*, if I had
> children and a family life, because I'd want to
> put my all into it and it is stressful, and you
> do get wrapped up in it. If you're really in the
> 'deep end' and you're really putting your *all*
> into it -and that's what I *would* want to do at
> some point- it makes family life difficult.

For a thirtysomething, Andreas, just completing his final
year, the course disappointed as it was utterly bereft of
political input.

> I think there's a core of very politically-
> minded people who are kind of a little bit
> disappointed and it seems to have gathered

momentum. Then there's the other half for whom it doesn't seem to matter. *This was about getting a job, one that looks like you'll never be out of work in.* You know, and you can do whatever you want. So I think there're two different types. I think those who've *engaged* with the degree, those who've truly engaged, are disappointed. Because they've engaged with it and feel a little bit let down that they've engaged with it and other people have been allowed to kind of just ease along on it.

When we do our PQ's [post-qualifying education] it will be just another process of coming here, doing it and going back to this other world, *the real world*, if you like. And I'm not up for that.

Developing as a person over the course of the degree

Students were asked how they'd changed over the 3 years of the degree: and to what extent any changes were due to the educational process, and to what extent were they 'natural' changes of maturation?

Chris, 23, sees the changes in her life as somewhat inevitable.

> *The course was great, it gave me time to get older.* And with that, unfortunately, comes more respect, because society is ageist.

Between 18 and 22 who doesn't change?
Everyone changes. Everyone changes, no matter
what, even if they say they *don't* change.
Because you learn so much more, you learn
to open your mind to things a bit more. I
remember having lectures about 'don't pre-
judge somebody when they walk into the
room.' That's part of how we figure out who
we are: 'I'm not like them, I would like to be
like them, I want to dress like them, I don't like
them, you know, whatever.' Then obviously
when we're working, you meet those people
and you get to know those people and you get
to know their troubles. *You just become a more
open and understanding person, I think.* So even
just in that respect -regardless of the actual
modules taught- being on the course with
people, living university life like all the other
students, you're going to change.

One 22 year old, Ali, felt the course gave her the time to
'mature.'

Yeah, I'm definitely a different person. I can't
necessarily put all of that onto the course,
because obviously I was 19 and now I'm 22.
Everyone changes when you grow up a little
bit. Also living away from home for so long
also changes you. But I definitely changed.
I'm a lot more mature - I wasn't *immature*,
but now I can make my own choices and
know why I've made them. Obviously in
social work practice I think I've come a huge

> way: from my first year, when I didn't have
> a clue, whereas now I can say, 'I've made this
> choice and I can base it on my professional
> judgement.' I'm confident in saying that,
> whereas I wouldn't have been able to say that
> last year and I think I've also learnt how to
> study a lot more.

Kolo, 33, a final year student and from an ethnic minority background, believes the course has made him more disciplined in life.

> I've become more *strict*. I think more than just
> as a social worker. Before I do *anything in life*
> I have to do a *risk assessment* [laughs]. So, in
> terms of friends and families, the way I talk to
> them, I talk to them very differently.

Three students point to the somewhat *inevitable* conflicts between the responsibilities of personal and family life versus the demands and commitments of the course. Firstly, Lauren.

> It's changed the way I think about things. I
> see things from very much more a social work
> *balanced* point of view and I *analyse things* more
> in my day-to-day life.

Rhiannon, 27, is a mother, and it is this aspect to her life that she highlights.

> I'm not quite as nurturing towards my kids as
> I was three years ago [laughs]. It's been really
> tough these last few months, so I haven't been

spending an awful lot of my energies on being
'mum,' the one that looks after everything that
needs to be done.

And, third year, Alexandria, 39.

Probably not having as much time at home
at the moment: my husband has to have the
children a lot, especially since I've been on
placement. I haven't seen him much really,
or as much as I would've done, and you find
you're preoccupied all the time, so I don't think
that's been a great thing. But then having such
long holidays makes up for the fact that you're
incredibly busy for a few weeks.

Perhaps a male student, Michael, in his final year and in his
40's, conveys a general view.

I think there was a steep learning curve.
A lot of people have changed and it's
opened a lot of people's eyes. But your quilt,
your comfort blanket, is a nice place to be
and wrap yourself up in: the little quilt of
ignorance. It's easy to slip back into that. Some
people will manage it better than others, but
what you have to hope is that at the end of
this -when they eventually get back into the
workplace- some of those little bells will be
triggered again. That's all you can do. *On
the job training afterwards, good support, good
supervision, that's what will do it, not another year
[of PQ training] here.*

The 'idea' of social work

One of the questions asked of the students was whether or not their 'idea of social work' had changed, significantly or otherwise, whilst undergoing their education and training.

Hayley, a 23-year-old student in her final year, posits a commonly-held observation.

> I think on the *placement* - seeing the social
> worker role and seeing it on a day-to-day
> basis- I think *that* has made me much more
> informed, and have a less fantasised idea about
> the role.

Q. You say you 'fantasised about the role.' What was the
    fantasy? Social workers as the fairy godmother?

> Yeah, definitely that. All these abused children,
> I'd take care of them, I'd protect them. Yeah,
> I mean I did, *I thought I could change the world*
> *and be this fairy godmother to service users*, but
> you're working for bodies that fund you, they
> resource how you work, and it's amazingly
> difficult to do good with all those constraints
> in your way.

Another final year student, Chloe, 23, makes a more unusual observation.

> I came to this university to do a degree in
> social work because you know what, to do
> social work, you need to have a degree. That's

the only reason. *But, actually, I truly don't believe
that you can teach social work.* I think you can
learn it and I think you can be open to being
taught it, but I don't think you can teach it
and the degree is set, in my view, to *teach* social
work. So it fails at that level.

To me it's about education predominantly
being a *two-way process.* An idea is put out
there: you take that idea, you either internalise
it, reject it, you work with it, do what you
want with it. It's not that you take an idea
and plant it on someone and then ask them
to write about that idea. Because then you're
then just producing an essay for a lecturer. I
hold my hands up and say I've done it.

When I'm talking about my experience, what
I enjoyed was the meeting of people, the
interaction that you get with people you get
on well with. And you kind of think they
think the same way as you. You talk. *I think
more social work is talked about in this university
by the students in the pub than is actually taught.*

Another final year student, Paul, 39, has definitely had his
ideas changed over the duration of the degree.

My idea of social work has changed
somewhat, but not a lot. I read the papers,
I knew the pressure, I knew who Victoria
C was before I came here and I knew all
the Met stuff, you know, Stephen Lawrence

and institutional racism. I've experienced
that from newspapers and from lying on the
pavement getting the crap kicked out of me.
*But what's changed is that it's far harder to actually
do the social work job than even I had considered
it was.* And every report or inquiry that's
written seems to make it harder. Free up the
police to spend more time on the streets, yes,
that's a good idea, but no no. Free up social
workers to spend more time with clients? No,
get them to tick little boxes.

It's a job, with an element of vocation thrown
in for good measure to keep the interest going.
But it's still just a job.

Anna, 30, however, appears not to have changed her views
that much.

[Laughs] It's all sorts of things. It's helping
people make changes in their lives, it could
be safeguarding people whether they're adults
or children. My line of work is safeguarding
adults, and another part of the work I do is
getting services for people and helping people
get through to the services - you know, find
the right pathway through the services to get
what they want.

I now have a deeper understanding, yes.
Although when I started I did have a very
strong feeling that I wanted to support carers
and help people feel better about the situation

they were in - because most of the work I
do is with people with dementia and that's
a hopeless kind of situation to be in. So I
wanted to think that I could help people to
see things more positively and to help people
get things that were good for them.

Marion, 27, holds a general, well-held view, of what the
social work role entails.

For me, I think it's about maximising the
potential of children, given their circumstances
and helping families through any kind of
adversity. Dealing with people who are
difficult people, dealing with everybody fairly
and I think as a social worker you can't afford
to be judgemental.

With the benefit of hindsight, Sylvia, 32, expresses a number
of opinions in her discussion of how she now perceives
social work.

A lot of people seem to want to do this job
to help people and I feel that that might be
slightly *delusional,* and perhaps they don't
actually realise what it's like. I think some
people might have a fanciful idea of what
social work is, and not a very realistic one. But
I think everybody has a genuine and deep set
reason for coming on this course.

Q. Why did *you* take the degree?

I saw it as a way to expand on what I'd done
before and to have more choice on areas to
work in: if I got bored after 5 years, I could
change into a different sector. I saw them
as quite clearly defined areas -older people,
younger people, mental health, disabilities- I
saw them as quite clear groups. I didn't really
think about the actual day-to-day gritty part
of social work.

*I think there's some truth in the idea of social work
being a temporary band-aid plaster, and I think
perhaps the government have a lot to answer for
because they give so much paperwork that it gives
you very little time to actually do good.*

I've been surprised by the clients I've been
faced with on my placement, because I think
it's very easy to make assumptions, and think
that it's just poorer-educated, lower class families
with less money. These are the sorts of things
that *would*, for example, increase the risk of
things like domestic violence or mental illness,
but the *breadth* of people I've met on placement
has really surprised me - and now I'm sure
there are people in other classes that are
suffering too. And particularly in an area such
as mental health, the breadth of that is going
to be wider than I think most people assume.
For example, for domestic violence clients, it's
not just single mums at home that've met a
complete waster of a bloke - there's a GP's
wife on the books and that really surprised me.

Q. Because?

> Because they're educated, they should know
> better, so I think that's probably what surprised
> me the most. You know, they're people who
> might be managers in very large companies, and
> it just makes you think they should know better.

Q. Do you think the course admitted the right kind
of student?

> *I don't think the key is admissions, because I don't
> think you can always really tell what a person's like,
> and even after three years you can't teach people to
> have empathy and to listen, and to have these skills.
> There are some skills you can't teach people to have,
> and if they don't have them, then I don't think
> they'll be particularly good at their job.*

> I think it's just a *very different* kind of job. I
> think it's quite an isolating job. Speaking to
> a child protection social worker yesterday,
> she was saying that a lot of her friends don't
> understand what social workers do and partly
> they don't *want* to know, because there're a
> lot of things that we see as social workers that
> many people would choose *not* to see. And
> she said that it's hard for her to relate her job
> to her friends, so actually many of her friends
> *are* social workers. And I found that even since
> doing the course -because it's all about social
> work when you're doing the course- it's hard
> for other people to relate to my job, so you

rely on the support of other students around
you. So I feel that I've moved away from a lot
of my other friends purely because they don't
understand.

Denise, 31, has been quite surprised by what she has
inadvertently learned about social work practice.

> *It has sort of surprised me just how lapse it is.*
> You're not supposed to take people's notes
> home, but they write reports at home,
> therefore they must have the notes at home
> with them if they're writing court reports at
> night, they must have these people's details.
> They shouldn't be carrying them around: you
> either have a rule or you don't. It seems to be
> that the rule applies if you feel like applying
> it. And people talk about their clients to other
> people which, okay, it might be professional,
> but I thought you were only meant to divulge
> this information *if it was important to do so.* Not
> just for general chit-chat. I don't think these
> people's feelings are taken into account.

Charlie, as she explains, sees the social work role as one of
enabling others.

> I think in some ways it's like greasing the
> wheels of everything else. You know, it's going
> back to how I thought of myself beforehand,
> you know, making sure everyone gets along
> to try and work together. I think social
> workers play a very critical role in trying to

get everyone to work together and look at
the whole situation rather than just what the
current or presenting problem is.

Rachel, 24, also focuses on the enabling role.

What is social work? I think it's -I mean
in relation to children, because that's what
I'm doing- helping a family access services
in order for them to avoid breaking up. Or,
like empowering and enabling people, so that
they can find ways to do things on their own.
So, not actually giving someone something
or telling someone 'this is what you need to
do,' but letting them find out on their own. I
think that's a big part of social work. *I also
think that nowadays there's a lot of paperwork.*

I know why I'm doing it so I don't need the
security of people liking me. In fact I don't
mind people not liking me, at all. It does put
me off child protection just because I think
maybe the organisational structure isn't in the
right place.

Simone, 30, tells a similar story.

I think social work is about supporting
people. Whether it's about making links or
signposting them, or direct work with children
and families or sort of short-term or long-
term intervention, just to help families with
the areas of need they've identified: whether

it be to improve their housing situation or
parenting skills, whether it be for the young
people to attend education or to get to and
from school, or to see the point in education,
to help maybe the parents deal with their own
issues they have or have had in the past.

Susan, 27, reflects on the *changes* in her perception of the
social work role.

My experience of social workers was probably
what I'd seen on *Grange Hill*. Nobody I
knew had any contact with social workers. It
just wasn't a profession I'd considered until I
happened to get a job, totally coincidentally, as
a clerk in a social services department.

I've not always been in childcare: I was an
assistant social worker, I was an adult social
worker in mental health. But the principles
are the same, it was helping a vulnerable
section of society getting their voices heard
when perhaps they couldn't do it themselves.

Students were encouraged to discuss how they felt the public
viewed social work and social workers, especially in the
light of the media furore over the death of Peter Connelly,
the public outcry and the implications for social work
intervention. Of course, to an extent, the reaction to the
Peter Connelly case was predictable. At the time, the most
commonly used *negative* words to describe social workers,
were failed/failure, bully/bullying, incompetent, bungling,
politically correct, shamed/shameful/shameless, arrogant,

betrayed, while the more *positive* descriptions included overloaded/overstretched/overworked, short-staffed, under pressure, demoralised, isolated, pilloried, recruitment crisis, too easy to blame social workers (*Community Care*, 2009:16).

Shirley, 23, a first year student, has no doubts as to how her chosen profession is perceived and described.

> I think it's scapegoating, it's what sells
> newspapers. Good news doesn't sell, and
> it's like if a doctor kills someone then it's in
> the newspaper. But you don't see all the *good*
> things that people do. And I suppose I'm quite
> lucky with my family because they don't buy
> into a lot of that stuff. My grandfather would
> probably be the worst, and probably because
> of his age, he's going to be quite biased and
> just believe the newspapers. He doesn't really
> understand what social workers do: he thinks
> that I'm going to work with old people and I
> haven't really corrected him on it, because he's
> too old to *understand*. But most other people
> I know are aware that a lot of it's [media
> coverage] fabricated and a lot of it's false. I
> would say that my partner's mum buys into a
> lot of it, she gets quite concerned and quite
> upset about some of the things that happen.
> She sort of takes everything incredibly
> seriously and I think the media should take
> more responsibility for what they do.
>
> Even on my placement some people have
> made it clear that they try not to say 'bloody

social workers' out of respect for the fact
that they've got students, but sometimes
they'll have a social worker who they deem
to be completely useless, and I think there
are social workers out there who aren't
particularly good at their job. I think that
it's unfortunate that they're not caught out
earlier, or somehow manage to slip through
this net of being completely useless. *It's not*
surprising that if other professionals have had a bad
experience with social workers then they're going to
think we're all the same.

Grace, 28, a final year student, is guarded about sharing what she does with other people.

I think there's a lot of stigma attached to social
work. I don't tell a lot of people I'm a social worker.
I pick and choose who I tell, because I don't think
it's something you want to advertise. Part of
me's very proud I've become a social worker,
but the other part of me…[sighs]…I'm not
embarrassed by it, but it's just something that I
choose not to advertise.

Ella, 24, was appalled by some of the things she'd heard from 'other professionals' about social workers.

Even a doctor the other day said, 'oh, what
do you want to be a social worker for? You're
all like Rottweilers – except Rottweilers
give children back,' and he laughed, all
this sort of thing. It amazes me, really, just

how short-sighted people are, even fellow professionals. I just think that people don't know enough about it, because all that's put in the newspapers is either, 'someone took the child away or they didn't take the child away.' But I think also too much is said in the workplace as well - 'we haven't got enough social workers, we're so short of staff, there's too much paperwork.' I've noticed that if they just got on with it a little bit more and stopped moaning about how short staffed they were, and how much paperwork they've got, a lot more would get done.

David, 36, a second year student, puts an interesting spin on the issue.

> *Social work, at this minute, is more likely to be changed than at any other time because no one values it.* That's why it's really important that the *politics* start coming back up again [sic]. *We are 'wankers,' we're the failures. We're either the people who take your kids away, or we're the ones that don't do nothing* [sic]. Social work has nothing to lose at the minute, and that's why it needs to try something new. Because there's nothing else to lose, because it's been eroded and eroded and eroded, and it's time now to reinvent what it is and to be realistic about it.

On reflection, many students expressed the opinion that the degree was insufficiently *practical*, and that they felt that they would benefit from practice-related learning at university, like report writing and knowledge of agency procedures and administrative formats.

Some students considered the degree to be "too easy" and, unsurprisingly, a number of them believed that recruitment would increase if the course length was reduced from 3 years to 18 months, or so. Indeed, a related issue -the pressures of family responsibilities and financial constraints- was highlighted by many interviewees. The social work degree, with its substantial practical component, requires a commitment that may indeed create familial and financial difficulties.

A number of respondents expressed the opinion that social work was even *more* complex and challenging than they had hitherto believed. Not only was it believed to be a job that required considerable commitment, some students questioned whether it could in fact be *taught*. Perhaps an individual had to be inherently or innately hard-wired for the job?

Students responded somewhat conventionally to questions about their changing ideas of what social work was: namely, that it was about supporting people, helping children, adults and families access services and, at times, engaging in direct face-to-face work.

Students expressed disquiet at disclosing their job to strangers, acutely aware of the widespread public condemnation or distrust of social work. They were aware, especially in the context of child protection issues, that social workers were almost placed in *Catch 22* situations - damned if they take children away, and damned if they don't.

Finally, there was an expressed belief that post-2010 was a watershed moment for social work. Change could occur, if there was the will to make it happen.

Chapter Six

Bureaucracy, multidisciplinary working, and newly qualified social workers

Bureaucracy

> There's a lot of paperwork, but I also think so much of a big thing is made of there being 'so much paperwork.' If you just *did it*, it'd just be easier. If you want to do a job like this, it can't be nine-to-five. So, if that means you have to stay late to get all your paperwork done, then that's one of the things that you're going to have to do. I think you've got to be prepared to do that, if not, *go and work in a shop.*

Carol, 27, final year student.

Max Weber (1864-1920), the German polymath -economist, historian and lawyer- whose social theory shaped much of modern sociology, believed that the rise of the 'rational rule-bound society' characterised by large-scale bureaucratic organisations, however initially successful, would eventually usher in the dystopian nightmare of the 'polar night of icy darkness.' Human creativity would be trapped inside an 'iron cage' of rule-bound control, and Weber believed that human societies would resemble gigantic bureaucratic offices (see Gerth and Mills, 1948). The whole world would ultimately resemble one enormous *office*. For Weber, the increasing bureaucratisation of social life formed the major structural form of modern capitalism: "rationalised efficiency which results from bureaucratic organisation enables humanity to develop economically and politically, but this progress is achieved at some cost, 'a parcelling out of the human soul,' a dehumanisation of the subject" (Swingewood, 2000:109).

Weber outlined the key characteristics of a bureaucracy, in the following manner. There would be:

- specification of jobs with detailed rights, obligations, responsibilities, scope of authority.

- a system of supervision and subordination.

- unity of command.

- extensive use of written documents, with no room for ambiguity.

- in-house-training-on-the-job and the requirement of certain skills.

- the application of consistent and complete rules (including, sometimes, a company manual), designed to enhance speed and precision.

- the assignment of work and the recruitment of personnel based on competence and experience.

In the 21st century, bureaucracies may be considered as inefficient, but in Weber's era they were seen as exceedingly efficient *machines* that reliably accomplished the aim of the organization. Certainly, bureaucracies are better for some tasks, than others: not well-suited to industries in which technology changes rapidly or is hitherto not well-understood, but good at where there are *routine tasks* that can be well-specified in writing and resistant to rapid change.

Critics suggested that Weber ignored much of what *actually went on* in organizations including, for example, the conflicts, the cliques, the deliberate avoidance of rules and, of course, the chain of command. *Within the context of social work*, the situation within agencies (social work organisations) is complex: sometimes individual autonomy does in fact require scrutiny and control, while at the same time the ability of managerial activity to control individual behaviour is invariably overstated.

The central critique of Weber's model is, however, that fundamentally, bureaucracies are *not machines* because they consist of human beings who, most of the time, do *not* imitate machines, and tend to possess the capacity to act *unpredictably*.

Deskilling and information technologies

A related and subsequent process to the evolution of bureaucracies is that of *deskilling,* described with clarity and passion in Harry Braverman's 1974 book, *Labor and Monopoly Capital: The Degradation of Work in the Twentieth Century.* Deskilling is the process by which skilled labour is eliminated by the introduction of technologies operated by semi-skilled or un-skilled workers. This results in cost savings, a re-definition of the work involved and, significantly, the reduction of the bargaining power of various workers. Deskilling may also decrease the quality of the work involved and *demean* the worker by reducing previously conceived 'cognitively creative' work to mere mechanical or repetitive work.

It is absolutely *unquestionable* that since the 1970's when individual decision-making, relative autonomy and individual creativity were an aspect of it, social work has increasingly become both bureaucratised and deskilled.

In their helpful analysis of the development of information technology within children and families departments, Shaw et al. describe how New Labour "initiated a radical programme to redesign the apparatus of government through the use of information and communication technologies," and how policy interventions for children in need were eventually brought within this apparatus" (2009:614). They describe how concerns about "insufficiently early intervention, perceived failures of children's agencies to recognize and respond to risk, and failures of information sharing between the professionals combined to prompt state intervention" (2009:614). The ICS [Integrated Children's System] is a government-led initiative and part of a wider package of developments for children's services, designed to promote effective services for children and families in England and Wales.

The ICS aims to help social workers and their managers 'assess, plan, intervene and review' in a systematic manner, and to enable them to collect and use "information systematically, efficiently and effectively" (Shaw et al., 2009:614). It's intended to apply to *all children in need* in England and Wales (about 370,000 at any one time), and not only 'looked after' children (about 60,000), or those on nationally required and locally maintained 'child protection registers' (about 26,000). Importantly, the ICS is "intended to be *at the heart of statutory child-care practice* in England and Wales" (Shaw et al., 2009:614, italics added).

Research undertaken among staff in three local authorities with experience of the ICS, initially *welcomed* the idea of a common computerized system and saw its *potential* for communicating information across agencies, although this potential, it was believed, was yet to be realized (Shaw et al., 2009:619). Moreover, "many thought that the ICS *took up time that would be better spent with their clients* and were very critical of it," arguing, for example, that the "tick boxes (e.g., 'client has mental health problems') were often irrelevant and too imprecise to be useful" (Shaw et al., 2009:619, italics added). The computerised forms were, the respondents argued, too complex to share with families and children or other professionals, and not particularly user-friendly. As one social worker remarked, "*what is lost in that is the child. You don't get a picture of the child and their needs very succinctly. It is all lost in these questions and jargon. It is very difficult for another professional to read it and get a picture of the child*" (Shaw et al., 2009:619, italics added).

Over and above the aforementioned problems, there were more 'basic' problems too: "users reported problems over complex logging-on procedures, entering data, finding data located on different screens, reading screens that flickered or were too small, crashing systems and remote access," and as such social workers maintained parallel paper files, as they "could not scan in letters and reports and were unable to sign off documents or transfer data securely by electronic means" (Shaw et al., 2009:621).

Shaw et al. assert that the "desire for a systematic evidence-based approach is reflected in a pressure to describe individuals in terms of *pre-determined categories* that are held to apply to everyone," which was seen as "leading to an unhelpful 'one size fits all' approach" (2006:623, italics added). For example, it is simply insufficient for a social worker to fill in the tick box 'problem drinking/drug misuse.' Instead, they may well need to know "when the person drinks, what happens, who may be in the house, what commitment the drinker may have to give up, whether he or she has tried before and much else besides." In conclusion, Shaw et al. argue that, insofar as the "information is covered, it is fragmented and in different parts of the forms," and insofar as "good practice depends on [such] detailed analysis," the ICS "cannot ensure it" (2009:623).

The research undertaken by David Pithouse and his colleagues reaffirms this view in their analysis of the *electronic* Common Assessment Framework. In essence, the CAF [Common Assessment Framework] is a voluntary arrangement that seeks to promote and enable practitioners, children, young people, parents and carers to *share information* about actual or potential needs and co-operate to try and deliver solutions to meet them. Of course, completing a CAF may not *necessarily* lead to inter-agency contact: "much will depend upon the nature of the needs and wishes of participants and whether the current services can be re-configured to meet the needs identified," but in principle it *can* "be used to establish contact with other agencies,

jointly develop plans and help to identify a lead professional"
(Pithouse et al. 2009:600).

Pithouse *et al* acutely summarise the concerns that've
been raised about state-sponsored ICT [Information
and Communication Technologies] systems in children's
services: "inappropriate surveillance and net-widening,
threats to citizen privacy, data security and quality, and
the unreflective assumptions within policy about universal
technology systems, such as CAF, to engage effectively with
the complexity of child and family needs" (2009:601). In
a similar vein to Shaw et al.'s findings, Pithouse also points
to some more 'basic' and elementary problems. As he and
his colleagues suggest, the implementation of the CAF is
based on a view of the social worker "having both the skills
and resources of an electronic office," assuming internet
access, electronic files and the space to work at the computer
in private, yet their research suggests that "completing an
e-CAF requires uninterrupted access to the internet for
at least an hour," and yet only 59 per cent [of 82 social
workers interviewed] considered the computer they used
was situated in a "quiet and confidential space" (2009:603).

Pithouse et al. conclude that, of course, "for many child
welfare professionals, their work is seen essentially as relational,
located in the home visit, clinic or classroom. Office tasks, by
contrast, have long been seen as an unwelcome distraction,
particularly where such tasks have an audit or controlling
function that undercuts worker autonomy" (2009:603).

Ferguson and Lavalette are more robust in their criticism
of computerised technologies, and argue that the ICS's
"onerous workflows and forms compound difficulties in
meeting government-imposed timescales and targets," and
that social workers are "acutely concerned with performance
targets, such as moving the cases flashing in red on the

screens into the next phase of the workflow within the timescale". As they put it, "*switching off the flashing red light bears no relationship to protecting a child*" (2009, italics added). Ferguson and Lavalette suggest that while the ICS records for Peter Connelly may well have been complete, and up to date, "the time required to complete such records is likely to have reduced the time available to carry our direct work with the family and reflect on the very complex issues involved in such cases" (2009).

Finally, and in Braverman-like language, Ferguson and Lavalette assert that as the focus of social work has become "entirely procedural", and that the *meaning* of the work has been lost and the needs of children have become secondary to the needs of agencies responsible for protecting them: "the contents of assessments appear insignificant as agencies are far more concerned about whether they are completed on time" (2009).

So, in respect to IT, what were the experiences and opinions of the participants? Debbie, a recently qualified social worker, describes the situation as she saw it.

> *I spend my entire life in front of a computer.* And the reason I have so many hours owed to me is because you either make a choice to sit in front of the computer or you see your children [clients]. And to do both, you have to work all the hours God sends. So I work in the evenings, I work weekends, I come in on bank holidays, *just* to keep my paperwork up to date. And it's still never up to date, but if I don't do that I don't spend time with my children [clients].

Q. Did this level of bureaucracy appear to emerge all
    at once?

> No, there was a build up to it. They moved
> to ICS and then to the ERIC system, as it is
> now, and ERIC has completely blown our
> paperwork out of the water. And it's not so
> much the quantity -the number of forms
> don't seem to have increased – but rather
> the *kind* of the way the computer system is
> designed. You have to go through 8 *processes*
> just to do one form, whereas before you could
> just do one form. There was a slight gradual
> build up to it, but they're not user-friendly,
> they're not in WORD formats. The training
> for it is difficult – it's okay if you're computer
> literate, but for some of my colleagues who
> are twenty years older than me and who really
> aren't interested in it, they're having a much
> harder time.

Richard, 28, a student approaching the end of his second
year, describes a similar situation.

> In the placement I'm in at the moment,
> which isn't the worst, there're *just far too many
> forms*, far too many. The manager in place
> at the moment is a very trusting manager,
> but she's just left! So you'd text and ask for
> a short stay placement for somebody, you
> know, a respite placement, and she'd agree
> it and if she couldn't get to the phone she'd
> agree the placement by text. She'd trust your

judgement, but obviously I'd then have to
go through my assessor. But her competent
and confident management has freed it up,
although you still had to go back and do all
the paperwork *afterwards*.

Emma, 37, a final year student, highlights the potential
adverse consequences of excessive bureaucracy.

*Statutory social work is massively target driven. If
you're working in children's services you don't spend
any time with the children.* You just about get
your stat visits in - you know, every 10 days
you're supposed to go and visit children on
plans, but sometimes the department hasn't got
the staff to do it.

Such complaints are neither novel nor recent. Adrian
Sinfield, writing in 1969, recalls a detailed study of
the 'child care service' in 7 Scottish local authority
departments, carried out in 1960, which found that the
social workers "spent less time than they estimated on
what they regarded as their major functions and more
time than they thought on other activities" (1969:22). In
particular -and recalling 'Emma's' disappointment at her
inability to actually meet children- most of the time was
spent travelling, administration and paperwork. In contrast,
"preventative work only took up one-tenth of the time,
children being received into care absorbing the greatest
amount of work." Sinfield concludes that "less than 2 hours
a week was spent with children and only about one hour
in conversation with them"(1969:22).

Multidisciplinary or interprofessional working

One of the consistently repeated assertions from the various post-1950's reports and inquiries into child deaths is that there's both a failure of communication and a lack of effective multidisciplinary working between various agencies like social work, education, health and the police, and that it's imperative that such working *becomes routine and effective.*

Final year student, Lily, 29, describes in considerable detail her experience of so-called multidisciplinary working.

> *Multidisciplinary working isn't working in statutory social work.* The team I was in -*in my third year-* meant I had to work alongside or work in partnership with education, health and housing services. *What a nightmare.* No one talks to each other [laughs]! People write reports, yet no one bothers looking at them, and then they'll turn up to meetings and they'll be like, 'well I don't really know anything about this.' *No one communicates with each other. They communicate via email occasionally, but there's no follow up.*

Q. I gather that you want to talk about the Common Assessment Framework?

> Yes, the Common Assessment Framework [CAF] is the big way now for social services targeting families before they get to *crisis.* So they'll set up CAF for young people and sometimes, on a lower level, TACs ['Team

Around the Child']. Basically, this means multidisciplinary teams getting together to work out the best solution for a child. This is all well and good, but nobody wants to take on the responsibility for *starting* one. I had a child that I'd been working with, who was in the 'looked after system.' I'd managed to get him back home with his mum and so needed to find him a new school, housing, and all those types of things. The services I provided to the family were actually becoming quite low level so he was put on Section 17 -which is a 'child in need'- and it enabled us to still offer some support to him. But then the aim was to close his case. I personally felt that the case *shouldn't* be closed, because I still felt there was a bit of work to do, especially with their benefits and finances. They were getting housing benefit and all those types of things, but hadn't actually come in at the point I was leaving, and I felt that, if that didn't happen, the mother probably wouldn't have the knowledge to go and sort it out [sighs]. So, I wanted to raise a CAF. The biggest issue for the child wasn't the housing, it was his education, as he was actually skipping school and his biggest problem was that he couldn't adjust to being at a new school.

Q. So what did you do?

I organised a meeting with education: we had SENCOs [special educational needs co-ordinators] there. They're almost like a mini-

social worker for children within schools
- you know, they identify children who need
some kind of assistance. SENCOs would
run a team around the child meeting for
instance. So…[pauses]…they were all there
and I mentioned that actually I felt that a CAF
was a really good idea for this child and that
Education would be the lead professional -
because for a CAF you need a lead professional
to take it on and from then on in, everyone
else reports to them. But nobody wanted it
- 'we haven't got the staff to do it, we're not
taking it on,' and I said, 'well, so what should
we do?' and they said, 'well, you need to raise
it, you're still working with him,' and I said,
'actually, I leave on Friday, so I can't be the lead
professional.' *But they really wanted me to sort of
start one and then disappear.* I thought it was so
frustrating and irresponsible and I said that *they
had to raise it* and I left it with them.

You know, it all depends on the person. I've
worked with a school, for example, where
there was a fantastic partnership, purely
because the headmistress was really into
it. Some people are just lazy, to be honest,
and don't want to pick up any more work.
Or they've got too much work to take on
anything else.

Q. Do you think there's a kind of *hierarchy* among the so-
called professions?

Let's take them one-by-one. *Education.* Some of them look down on Social Services, but then they look down on the children they're dealing with, I think. You know, someone they simply don't want to have in *their* school. *Health Services.* It depends who you're talking to, really. I found that Health Visitors, Nurses, Midwives were always very communicative and actually multidisciplinary working with *them* was very good. But the higher the level you get to, the less communication you get.

Doctors are in their own little world. The only times I've encountered doctors were at adoption panels or when you try to gain information about children that've gone for paediatric assessments. They're not very forthcoming about giving you information, they just send a standard letter. I mean, some of them were sending letters to the family of the child, nothing to us, and we wouldn't even know if a child had gone and had a test done because you wouldn't get the results through. You *don't* send it just to the parents because they're not going to tell you anything. So unless you're very mindful and you know your cases very well, you could miss quite a lot, you really could. The only things you *do* get an immediate response from are when you send a child for tests about non-accidental injuries [NAIDs]. You get feedback straight away. But other things… [well]… let me give you an example.

There was a family with twin babies that
weren't developing. They were losing weight,
they went into the hospital, and the only
reason we found out *anything* was because
I was ringing the nurses on a daily basis.
Then you've got others who obviously
won't divulge information over the phone,
and quite rightly so. You have to give them
your details and say, 'could you call me back?'
Because obviously they don't know who you
are, but then they *don't* call you back. It's so
frustrating. I mean it is *really frustrating*.

Newly qualified social workers

The Task Force argues that, in addition to 'high quality'
practical placements, there should be a "new supported
and assessed first year in employment, which would act as
the final stage in becoming a full, practising social worker"
(2009:7). It is difficult to imagine how *in reality* this might
be achieved, given the severe budgetary constraints of local
authorities, the variation in the structure and resources of
other voluntary or charitable social work employers, and
the sensitive and varied relationships between individual
educational institutions and individual social workers.

Why did you decide to train as a social worker?

The first question *newly qualified social workers* were asked
concerned the reasons behind their choice of social work

as a career. Many of the answers, unsurprisingly, are similar to those of students undergoing training. For instance, Catherine, 27, focuses on her own biography as a reason for her motivation.

> Since I was fostered and adopted, I've always
> had a fascination with social workers and how
> they get involved in that process.

Emily, 42, also mentioned fostering, but in a somewhat different context.

> I wanted to be a foster carer for teenagers.
> However, I had no spare room so considered
> social work as an alternative.

Wanting to 'make a difference', was repeated by many of the newly qualified social workers, as in Chris's case.

> Having studied for 3 years as a nurse in
> learning disability, I wanted to compliment my
> knowledge and be able to make a difference to
> people in a kind of more integrated way.

Momona's own life experiences were a major factor in *her* career choice.

> Throughout my life I've supported and
> advocated for my family and friends. I've cared
> for my friends when they've been seriously ill.
> Also my twin sister had a serious illness and
> I've supported her throughout, whether just
> 'being there' or supporting her in accessing

various services. Sadly, my sister passed
away, but her illness gave me an insight into
discrimination, prejudice and stigma, not only
from individuals but also from services.

I wanted to *change the system*. I've had several
diverse life experiences that I've managed to
cope with, reflect on and then move on. I had a
terrible period of depression, domestic violence
and homelessness. The period of trauma allowed
me to rethink my career goals, and subsequently
through this, reinforced the idea that I can
become more pro-active. This has all helped in
my social work career, so far.

What were the highs and lows of social work education?

With the benefit of hindsight and the additional experience
of *actually* practising social work full-time, the newly
qualified social workers were asked for the 'highs and lows'
of their training.

Kate, 30, was quite critical.

The lows were the difficulty I experienced
with some of the subjects such as Sociology,
and the limited time spent on each subject.
In other words, the lack of depth given to the
subjects. Once qualified we should've had a
year of a *protected case load*.

On the course there was also a distinct lack
of support on placement. *The degree gives you
a flavour of many subjects and makes you multi-
skilled, but master of none.*

Theresa, 33, also discusses her somewhat unsatisfactory
placement experience.

I had a negative placement experience in my
second year. A day centre that *allegedly* provides
'work opportunities' for people with learning
difficulties. Well, I actually perceived it to be
slave labour for people with learning difficulties.

I also didn't enjoy the Social Work Methods
module, and I found the reading material for
that module very difficult to grasp.

Claire, 25, also points to difficulties with particular modules.

The Mental Health, Disability and Child
Protection modules were all too brief. All three
are vital subjects which appear to underpin
most areas of social work practice, yet were far
too brief. And there were simply not enough
lectures on Child and Adult Protection. Also,
there were a limited number of books in the
library for the number of people on the course.

And, I personally find it very difficult to stay
focused in lectures unless they are *interactive*
and hands-on.

Natalie, 24, focused on various issues of time management.

> I found it difficult to manage time when being
> on placement. In particular, writing practice
> and module assignments, while at the same
> time preparing a dissertation.

> For the dissertation I had trouble recruiting
> social workers to interview: I emailed and
> telephoned many times, and eventually had to
> ask a social worker colleague on placement to
> contact her friends in the locality office. As a
> result of this I had to request a late submission
> for my research project.

Lynne, 27, also had issues with time management.

> I felt under *constant pressure* from balancing
> work and study. And, at the same time, I was
> also nursing my mother who was suffering
> from dementia.

Jo's response to the question was brief, and to the point.

> *I found it a very depressing and difficult course.*

Samantha's problems with the degree were acutely *personal*.

> The *lows* were always at the point of having
> to write assignments when, at which time, I'd
> become paralysed by my childhood ghosts: feeling
> I was inadequate and stupid. I just felt such terrible
> emotional pain each time I was faced with essays.

Jen, 23, expressed a number of concerns and complaints.

> I felt there was a tokenistic attitude to some
> areas of social work (e.g., mental health),
> although I recognised this was not a university
> decision, but one led by GSCC guidelines.
> Also, a big complaint of mine was having a
> dissertation tutor who had little knowledge of
> the area of social work I was researching and
> writing about. *He was useless.*

Finally, Georgina, 29, returned to the subject of practice placements.

> The lows? Firstly, *difficult placements.* You know,
> having practice assessors who weren't able to
> communicate, empathise or who'd leave half-
> way through the placement [sighs]. *Finances.*
> Not being sponsored meant that even when
> working I had to go into massive debt. Sadly,
> the university hardship fund has chosen to
> use a system which means that 95 per cent of
> students couldn't get help.

Theory and practice

The newly qualified social workers were questioned about the perennial educational issue in social work training: had they found it difficult to relate theory to practice?

Tess, 37, comments on the lack of time in practice to *reflect* on actions.

> I think many social work decisions and actions
> are made quickly and you don't always think,
> 'oh that was solution-focused.' You just don't.

In a *written* response to the specific question, Gemma, 38, was confident about the application of one to the other.

> Initially yes, particularly after 'trying' to read
> Malcolm Payne. However, once I stopped
> reading him and looked at other books I
> realised I'd *always* been applying theory to
> practise [sic] but cud [sic] know [sic] name
> it, ie., task-centred, systems, and learnt about
> other theories that I've tried in my practise
> [sic] to apply.

Sian, 41, believed that 'theory' was absolutely essential.

> Since qualifying I've seen how essential
> this focus on theory is. It underpins any
> intervention I undertake and allows me to
> justify and reflect on my practice. *I* now have
> social work students and I constantly refer
> them to *theory* and ask them to state why and
> what theory they're using.

Annabel, 30, a newly qualified social worker, simply considered the process of relating theory to practice far too difficult. She found the theory she encountered on the degree difficult to comprehend.

> I felt it would've helped to have details of
> what *actually happened during casework*, and *then*

to discuss the theories that might have been
used alongside this.

And, I found 'studying' theory impossible to
understand, as I needed to relate it to real work.

Jan, 24, however, stressed the positive influence of the role
of the practice teacher.

With the assistance of an excellent practice
teacher I was able to implement theory
throughout my work.

In a 2010 survey of NQSWs [Newly Qualified Social
Workers], Bates et al. report on what such newly qualified
workers believed they were sufficiently equipped to deal with
compared to those areas of work they felt ill-prepared for.

These workers felt they were reasonably well-prepared for
the following.

- Communications skills, social work methods,
  responding to cultural differences, social work
  law, critical perspectives, evidence and research-
  based practice, social work values, working in an
  organisation, interprofessional working, and the
  role and responsibilities of a social worker.

Conversely, they felt less well-prepared to carry out the
following tasks, roles and responsibilities.

- Assessment, report writing, record keeping, time
  management, case management, dealing with

> conflict, and care management and contracting;
> court skills (Bates et al., 2010).

In other words, these newly qualified social workers felt inadequately prepared for the *core* tasks of social work, like assessment, report writing, court skills, and case and care management.

Did the course adequately prepare you for a full-time social work post?

Ava, 27, one of the newly qualified workers interviewed, was concerned in particular about Child Protection modules.

> The course only gave a quick overview of
> child protection [safeguarding], but needed
> to be extended with more case examples
> and possibly a role play situation involving
> other professions. Maybe a role play involving
> a strategy/case conference, as well as looking
> at child protection care plans in far
> more depth.

Miriam, 31, shares similar concerns.

> I feel that having time in exploring the role of
> core assessments in the children and families
> option would have been of great benefit to
> me, as I've never completed one.

Viv, 34, concurs, in respect of *adult* protection.

I don't think they [modules] were sufficient to practice in adult protection. Without further training and information, especially relating to the locality you're working in, it would be *very* difficult to practice safely.

The safeguarding adult sessions were too late in the course to have an impact on my practice. By the time we undertook this module I'd been part of a [level 4] investigation and therefore it was insufficient. *The safeguarding modules cannot fully prepare you for practice. More case studies would be useful so that students can explore processes more fully.*

Anna, 24, wanted more *relational work,* more training for working on a one-to-one basis with clients.

What I would've wanted was more time and in-depth study on counselling, psychology and working with people and families. And far less time on assessment, planning and reviewing.

Tina, 30, believed that processes and skills, like report writing, were understated on the degree.

I don't think the course prepared me for things such as writing court statements. In my post it's an expectation that social workers do the counselling for birth parents when they relinquish a baby – I simply don't feel prepared by the course to have the skills to do this.

However, I do feel the course taught me to remain *neutral in my thinking and to challenge things*. It'd be really good if the course had a module on helping someone write their 'life story narrative' as life story work is a big part of my role. *Also, I don't think the course covers enough of managing conflict.*

Olivia, 25, somewhat unusually, raises the issue of sponsored students.

As an independent student who wasn't sponsored I've felt in some ways discriminated against in the workplace. For example, when I first started in my team, 7 months ago, what was constantly mentioned was my 'lack of social work experience,' in comparison to the sponsored social workers in the same office. In addition, I was constantly challenged with – 'well, what *did* you learn at uni?' Interestingly, my line manager has said that she would've preferred someone with at least 2 years experience, especially in terms of familiarity with the paperwork and computer systems. However, within a 3 year degree course I cannot see how it could be changed to make a module to cover *all* aspects of paperwork.

Marian, 29, felt that the degree was biased towards social work with children and families.

I feel the course had little to do with the social work position I'm now in. I moved to

Adult Services and the course was *clearly*, *clearly*
oriented to Children's Services. Working with
children, not with adults.

Wendy, 33, felt that the academic side of the course was
overemphasised.

I feel that the education I received was
unbalanced. *There was far too much weight put
on turning 'skills' into an academic subject and not
enough value put on the practical part of the course.* It
seems absurd that people can write an essay and
get a better grade, but no matter how well you
actually practice, this isn't graded. *Just pass or fail.*

Finally, Sue, 25, mentions her own social work career *prior*
to training.

If I hadn't had years of *Assistant Social Work
experience* I'd be unlikely to have had the
confidence to take what I learnt in the
classroom into the actual workplace.

What was missing from the degree?

It might well be assumed that some newly qualified
social workers will *improve* their practice *over time*. Indeed,
Bates et al., paraphrasing other researchers, argue that the
"development of expertise is a gradual transition from a
rigid adherence to taught rules and procedures through
to a largely intuitive mode of operation in which learning
from experience is the main force of transition" (2010: 154).

Newly qualified workers were asked what they considered was absent from the degree, and what had been unnecessary.

Shirley, 39, made numerous suggestions.

> *I feel we needed so much more training in child protection in order to help us protect the children we're working with.* More on counselling people, is also needed. *Writing court statements. Court skills and witness skills.* More placement opportunities to help you make the decision about *where* you want to work.
>
> The ECDL [European Computer Driving Licence, the IT qualification] is unnecessary, in my opinion: if you can use WORD and the Internet you're okay. Finally, I understand the importance of 'reflection,' but don't feel we needed quite so many lectures on the subject [laughs]!

Evie, 29, reiterates some familiar themes.

> There's not enough covered on the *real world of social work*, i.e., poverty, squalid living conditions, poor health, death and dying. These're all very common factors in my role as a social worker in Adult Services. Also we need more sessions on the various work pressures – you know, paperwork, time management and stress. These need to be covered and discussed to give a taste of how pressurised the role can actually be. Also joint working with

Health and other areas and the differences and
difficulties this presents, and how often social
workers are left to pick up the pieces and
dumped upon - this is also very necessary.

But it's not discussed on the course.

Paul, 50, concentrated his views on the safeguarding modules.

The specialist adult modules, disability and
mental health, were far too short. Increased
teaching on safeguarding *is a must,* as it's taking
over statutory chores more and more. *There's
a lot of repetition in the course*, especially around
ethics and values.

Another male social worker, Gerald, 40, points to the
students' *emotional development.*

Much more time is needed in the care setting
in the first year. Possibly some time should also
be spent on the student's feelings and emotions
while in the first year. We weren't really
prepared for our second year placements, not
at all.

Pauline, 34, was concerned with what she saw as the lack of
a *thematic* approach to learning.

It would've been easier to relate to each subject
if all areas had been covered at the same time,
i.e., when working on disabilities to have a
session on the law in relation to disability and a

> session on the skills required for working with
> various disabilities. This would've made it more
> *real.* Also, how to use the relevant paperwork,
> i.e., report writing, and *maybe more about*
> *balancing the personal social work role with the role*
> *and priorities of the employer.*

Finally, Alicia, 30, reserves her criticism for her peers, as well
as the degree itself.

> All necessary subjects were covered but I feel
> more time could've been given to certain
> areas, for example, mental health, and also
> sessions with service users. I must also add, on
> a personal level, that role playing was in no
> way useful for me. It's extremely difficult to
> have the commitment of an entire group of
> students to a method of teaching like this, and
> without the input of *all* students it becomes a
> bit of a waste of valuable time.

Has social work lived up to your expectations?

In their study of newly qualified social workers working in
children and families teams, Gordon Jack and Helen Donnellan
report that, "whilst the social workers in the study all started
their first jobs as newly qualified professionals with optimism
and confidence, it was alarming to see how quickly these
feelings drained away in the face of the day-to-day reality of
the work they were required to do, and the conditions under
which that work was undertaken" (2010:316).

Although some of our participants had only been in post for less than 12 months we asked them whether social work had lived up to their personal expectations.

Mary, 30, was in no doubt.

> *Not at all.* Current social work is managerial and controlled by paperwork and statistics and performance. *I thought social work would be more specialist, about being with people and supporting them through the tough experiences of life rather than directing them to services where other people do that.* I never wanted to be a care manager who just directed people and organised services. I wanted to help and support people through the challenges they faced – to go with them on their journey to recovery, or change, or a better life. Anyone can learn to be a care manager, directing services, *but it takes a special person to be a social worker* who supports people through life's challenges and makes a difference to their lives.

Rosemary, 34, in practice for 10 months, concurred.

> The title *'care manager'* seems far more appropriate to me because that seems to be what the government really wants us to do – manage the professional and family networks, *not help resolve the real underlying problems.* The focus is on *monitoring*, and thereafter there isn't the time to do both. The job I think we *should* be doing is much more enjoyable and I believe would have much better outcomes for children.

Perhaps this distinction between 'care management' and 'real social work' is worthy of mention. To put it succinctly, Care Management is the principal *rationing instrument* of a fragmented and market-led care system. The emphasis is on accountancy and the monitoring of spend. It is also, allegedly, supposed to monitor quality. Some social work skills *may* be used in care management, but essentially the care manager organises the money and 'contracts' for someone else to do the *people-social-care-relational work*. In contrast, it may be argued that social work is a values, human rights and justice-led approach to handling *personal and* -potentially, albeit unlikely- *social change*. The emphasis is on respect for the unique predicaments of *individuals in context*, human relations and social justice. Some care management *may* be undertaken within social work. Social work is also, of course, an instrument of *state control* in terms of 'protecting' particular individuals from what is perceived to be potential harm, and also through *'keeping the lid' on potential community and social unrest*.

Bella, in her 30's, in post for some 6 months, finds her job both satisfying but also profoundly frustrating.

> I cannot think of anything nicer than choosing
> a family for a child and then the child being
> adopted by them: it is *so* rewarding. However,
> I do *not* enjoy managing so much conflict. I
> guess you can't always please everybody.

Fay, 37, personally discovered that social work was not such a welcoming environment.

> Whilst I didn't expect the red carpet treatment,
> I didn't think I'd be unsupported and treated

with hostile contempt. I got through this by
imagining scenes from the comedy *The Office*
and forming comedy characters out of the
worst offenders.

Social work is a great job. I love it. But, sadly,
it's becoming more and more about 'processes,'
paperwork and office-based work. However, I
still feel I make a difference.

Harriet, 26, is an unusual interviewee in that social work *has*
lived up to her own expectations. However, she does raise
the central and crucial issue of the 'eligibility' for various
services.

Yes [it's lived up to my expectations] but there
are, of course, some surprises along the way.
These are about *fair access in care services* where I
feel that some people who may have benefited
from social work are said to be *ineligible*
because they're slightly to the left or right of
the eligibility mark. This affects my ability
to deliver social work care as it's primarily
governed by the availability of funds.

Indira, 32, concludes this section and introduces the
subsequent discussion, through her account of her perception
of the modern social work role.

I feel there's a great contradiction, orchestrated
by local authorities and government, who
come up with well-meaning policies and
training, but then make it impossible for

social workers to exercise their 'power' and values to support, assist and work with and for service users. *Social workers spend more time managing budgets rather than people, and filling in forms to satisfy the target-driven element that is eclipsing effective working.* For example, showing someone that I've completed 20 pathway plans tells *me nothing*, apart from that I've met some target and ticked boxes. *We should be called social entrepreneurs.*

Bureaucracy at work

Many of the newly qualified social workers have already mentioned the increasing bureaucratization they encounter and confront: however, we asked them *specifically* about the issue.

Imogen, 27, is simply angry.

The current system restricts social workers from doing 'social work' - you know, actually being with people and helping them practically as well as emotionally. *Social workers are slaves to paperwork and statistics.* There's so much concentration on filling in forms and codes *in a culture of blame* instead of allowing social workers to actually be with people. My experience of practice is of constantly being told just to 'send information.' Even if there wasn't the money to pay for services, people still need to talk to a person face-to-face

who can support them through the potential
minefield. *In university we were taught the
ideal, not the reality*, and we should have been
prepared for being pen-pushers who could
handle saying 'no' to people because that's
what most of the work for councils involves.

Noreen, 27, also discusses IT and, in particular, a specific
system.

I didn't expect the confusion over the
county's computer system. This takes up
an unnecessary amount of a social worker's
time and leads to utter frustration. I love the
job, but would like to have more time with
mentors to explore policies and procedures to
support me in this confusion.

Jez, 34, discusses the IT situation in his London borough.

I spend about 75 per cent of my time on the computer.
I currently have to update two databases. It's
all duplicated nonsense. The amount of money
wasted on IT is absolutely incredible. I'm just
about to get my fourth computer in three
years. We had one computer set up 18 months
ago with a scanner which sits on its own desk
collecting dust. We were told we were going to
have to scan all our files, one page at a time, and
go *paperless* but no one mentions it any more
and no one's ever turned the scanner on! They
took away our desk phones a year ago and now
we have these shitty little mobiles.

The future of social work? It'll be to train up
unqualified staff to do the job cheaper and
take the can if anything goes wrong. Our team
has been cut by 60 per cent and we're being
integrated into the voluntary sector, which
will be shit.

My partner's also a social worker. She
manages a team of unqualified administrators
and assistant care managers, and she's like
'the brain' telling them what to do while
she manages the 700 referrals a month
across several databases and two screens, like
some city trader. *For fuck's sake!*

Post-qualifying [PQ] modules

Students, in their second and third year, are acutely aware
that on graduation they will continue their education and
training through undertaking PQ courses. Not all such
students welcome this development: indeed, final year
student, Richard, 43, is forthright in his assessment of the
PQ framework.

They've already split the post-qualifying
course to an Adults option or a Children's
option, so you make your decision and you're
committed for life. I disagree with that.
*Social work values should be generic - it's about
having time to see things. It's about 'reading people.'
Sitting people in here for another year isn't going to
make people more aware when they come out.*

Banging them over the head with a book isn't going to help. It's about having the time and the experience to look at people and their ability and their will to question things. Why has he got chocolate all over his face every time I come and visit? For God's sake, just get the flannel and have a look! But the PQ is 'jobs for the boys,' again isn't it? The GSCC [General Social Care Council] is another committee, another quango. *Just bullshit.*

The post-qualifying framework is part of the GSCC's drive to "equip a trained and trusted workforce," wherein social workers are "required to keep their skills and knowledge up-to-date" (GSCC, 2010). One way of updating 'skills' is by registering for a PQ award at a contributing educational institution. These awards are at three academic levels – specialist, higher specialist and advanced.

The Task Force is robust in its recommendation of a single, nationally recognised career structure, one which would "map each of the main stages of a career in social work from degree course entrant onwards, making clear the expectations that should apply to social workers at each of these stages; give shape to the more coherent and effective *national framework for the continuing professional development of social workers* which we are also recommending and which should incorporate the new Masters in Social Work Practice" (2009:8). Further, the Task Force recommends "a new *system for forecasting levels of demand for social workers,* which can eventually be used for local, regional and national planning concerning training and recruitment" (2009:8).

The *newly qualified workers* were asked if they had begun any PQ education. Kate, 32, expresses a common opinion.

> The PQ 'Consolidation' part was taught *in
> an almost identical way* to my undergraduate
> degree, which is why I found it fairly
> infuriating. I know it does what it says on the
> tin, and it *is consolidation,* but it felt a little like
> – '*hang on, I finished this in May and it's only
> September, you know.*'

Yvonne, 24, is in agreement.

> I'm not very clear as to the purpose of PQ
> modules so far. Unfortunately, I've found the
> content to be *repetitive* and have learnt very
> little new information with regards to theory
> and research.

> You know, it's very, very *repetitive* – with
> nothing new at all. Some teaching is of a very
> poor quality. *It's something necessary for the job:
> pay rises, career progression, that kind of thing.* But,
> writing essays, reading, etc., on weekends and
> evenings does not inspire enthusiasm for the
> course, especially when it's important to read
> up-to-date research and articles to ensure
> best practice.

Much of the impetus behind the evolution of the post-qualifying framework is the almost obsessive preoccupation for social work to acquire 'professional' status. There are conflicting processes at work: on the one hand, the occupation has been deskilled through the redefinition of social work as care management, yet on the other hand there is the desire for 'professional' status. And, like such occupations as law, architecture, accountancy and medicine, continuing professional development is seen as an essential element of such a sought-after status.

Professions not only claim an area of specialist and exclusive knowledge and skills, they also purposively create monopolies and deny access, knowledge and skills to others (Johnson, 1972). It's difficult to believe that social work -whether as social work or care management- truly possesses such areas of specialist and exclusive knowledge and skills: not only do social work departments employ non-qualified workers who carry out tasks almost *identical* to those of qualified workers, it is simply difficult to pinpoint any true *uniqueness* of knowledge, expertise and skill.

Supervision

In respect to newly qualified social workers, the Task Force insists that there has to be a "clear supervision policy," whereby they would expect "minimum frequency levels normally to be weekly for first 6 weeks employment, then fortnightly for the duration of the first six months," and after "six months in post, this would move to a minimum of monthly supervision, with each session at least an hour and a half of uninterrupted time." Finally, the Task Force insists that where the "line manager is not a social worker, professional support should be provided by an experienced social worker" (2009:22). It is surely reasonable to ask how they believe this can possibly be achieved, given the recruitment and retention problems that already exist and that will invariably continue.

To summarise: the social workers were asked about the amount and quality of supervision they received in their workplace. The majority of them offered wry responses -facial expressions rather than actual words or sentences-to the question, but perhaps Yvonne's response is somewhat representative.

> This has been an ongoing problem for 2 years.
> My current manager has been off sick again –
> this time for several weeks and with no date
> for his return. The service manager is covering
> my supervision and does try to make himself
> available, but it's not sufficient. Not at all.

Multidisciplinary or interprofessional working

Our newly qualified social workers were asked whether they thought social work would benefit from the outpourings of criticism following the Peter Connelly death and the various reports, inquiries and recommendations focusing on issues like the need to improve multidisciplinary working.

Ajit, 33, believes that the latest round of recommendations have in fact been potentially helpful.

> Yes, as its highlighted the lack of safeguarding
> knowledge in medical staff, and the *lack of
> communication between medical and social care.*
> More multidisciplinary joint working *was* a
> major issue. Managers not being from a social
> care background was *also* an issue. And not
> being believed or being heard was yet
> another issue.

Alice, 24, hopes that as a result of the inquiry that followed the death of Peter Connelly and the subsequent establishment of the Task Force, her workload will be eased.

> I hope it'll highlight the difficult job
> that social workers have, and that as a
> consequence caseloads will be reduced.
> However, I suspect that social workers
> will feel more *de-motivated and scared of the
> work* and this will lead to poor practice as
> practitioners will not want to take risks.

Linda, 30, positively values multidisciplinary or interprofessional working.

> I am highly pro-active when working with
> other professions. I value interprofessional
> working and am always looking to build
> relationships over time. However, I've
> found health services somewhat difficult to
> share information with - mental health in
> particular.

Viv, 27, believes that the process of joint working is down to particular individuals.

> In my experience, the efficiency at this kind of
> working is very much *personality-led*. Meaning,
> it's down to individuals within the setting to
> build networks and *behave in a manner* that
> promotes interprofessional working.

Bea, 25, concurs.

> I work in a community mental health
> team where there're nurses, doctors, OTs
> [occupational therapists], psychologists
> and social workers. In this team it's been
> a positive experience, where professionals
> share their skill set. In other CMHTs it's *not*
> worked so well, but I feel that was down
> to the manager of the team not respecting
> disciplines such as social work and OT.

Finally, Chantelle, 28, is positive, albeit with reservations.

> My experience of interprofessional working is
> *positive*. I choose to use every opportunity to
> be helpful with my colleagues and to foster an
> understanding of my own role, as well as learn
> about others. The most unfortunate part of
> this is that, no matter how hard you try, every
> professional or team has their own parameters
> to work in, and there's not enough flexibility.

The newly qualified social workers repeated many of the opinions and observations held and expressed by the students. For example, there was frustration at the increasing bureaucratization involved in much practice – "I spend my entire life in front of a computer." Similarly, both the 'target culture' and the predominance of managerial oversight was spoken of somewhat disparagingly. Of course, these issues are intimately related to the empirical fact of the transformation and re-configuring of social work into care management: indeed, many workers compared "real social work," when criticizing the deskilled role of 'care management.'

There was unanimity in opinion that on their prior degree courses there was a distinct lack of information, discussion and 'theory' in the field of adult and child *protection*. The workers believed that, essentially, on graduation they were ill-equipped for work in that particular field. They also believed that the students on the degree would benefit from there being more teaching about the various bureaucratic and computer *systems* they would encounter in the field.

There was also unanimity in respect of *supervision*: this was found to be inadequate in terms of time and frequency of contact, and of it not being given priority by their employing agency.

Again, in symmetry with the students, the newly qualified workers in principle valued the idea of multidisciplinary or interprofessional working, but in practice encountered obstacles. Whether or not such working was positive or fruitful was perceived to be dependent on the *individuals* involved and, additionally, a belief that certain professional cultures were more amenable than others. Finally, frontline workers in various sectors were considered to be more amenable than those in more managerial roles or with higher status.

Post-qualifying education was neither welcomed nor considered to be valuable: the consensus was that, from their experience of initial modules, it was something of a repetitive exercise, offering little in terms of new research, ideas or teaching innovation. It was a necessary activity to be endured, predominantly for potential career progression and personal financial benefit.

Chapter Seven

Conclusions: Which way for social work?

I can usually say, 'I don't work with children,' and that sometimes closes the book. The meaning of social work has just been pulled apart by the media, and it's not represented as something that can help and benefit someone. I've had people that I've not seen for a while go, 'oh, what are you doing with yourself these days, how've you been?' 'I'm a social worker.' They turn their back. *They actually turn their back on me.* Some people have had bad experiences with social workers and that's fair enough, 'cos when you come in at a really bad time in somebody's life you're not always going to get it right.

Chris, 25, a newly qualified social worker.

Managerialism and the reconfiguration of social work

Social workers continue to face enormous challenges: the high level of *societal abuse* directed against the poorest and most vulnerable individuals, families and communities, and the continued violence and abuse of adults and children in the home. The NSPCC data shows that while 'child homicides' are rare, the most likely culprits are family members. *Every ten days in England and Wales one child is killed at the hands of a parent*, compared with an annual average of 11 children a year killed by strangers. The statistics for sexual abuse suggest that 16 per cent of children under the age of 16 experience some form of sexual abuse, while 21 per cent of children experience some degree of physical abuse at the hands of their parents or carers (see the Child and Woman Abuse Studies Unit [CWASU]).

However, it is also important to note that the overall child homicide rate in England and Wales of around 67 child deaths per year appears to have remained broadly similar to the 1970's and may actually have decreased slightly (Ferguson and Lavalette, 2009). So, despite the endless castigation of social workers for 'failing to intervene' it is apparent that social workers have, given the adverse circumstances, probably been performing as well as could possibly be expected. Moreover, such raw statistics only offer a partial description and explanation of such events for while Home Office classifications tell us *how* a child was killed, they can only hint at the events leading up to the death and its possible prevention: "Cases where the children are killed by monoxide poisoning in a car on a custody visit by a 'loving' father who then commits suicide are very different from those where a child dies from multiple injuries, following a long period of ill treatment...[or]...where a lone mother, who has cared very well for her child in the past, starts showing increasing signs of mental disturbance and finally kills the child dramatically, in a psychotic outburst" (Ferguson and Lavalette, 2009).

Managerialism in social work emerged in the 1970's when the ideas of the 'market,' 'efficiency' and 'accountability' began to be applied to public services. Behind this development was an attack on the so-called 'dependency culture' wherein social workers and other public service workers were perceived to be somewhat 'self-serving,' controlling their own work, and *creating their own clients.* As a result, the decision was made to reform the Welfare State and introduce elements of privatisation and the principles of the marketplace. Integral to this was the emergence and privileged role of the *manager.*

The manager's role was to transform the Welfare State by measuring 'success' primarily in *financial* and not *welfare* outcomes. Social work was transformed into care management and, because of its weak standing and lack of 'professional identity,' social work leadership was unable to resist the changes.

The detail is instructive: a report by the Government's 'Efficiency Unit,' *Improving management in Government: The Next Steps,* published in 1988 and looking at the changes in the 'management of government business,' goes to the heart of the matter. It was the catalyst in creating government 'delivery' agencies which, operating within a 'general management framework,' worked with *plans, targets and performance management and review.*

The Report's authors argue that there had been an "insufficient sense of urgency in the search for better value for money and steadily improving services" (Jenkins, et al., 1988:1) and conclude that "the substantial gain we are aiming for is the release of managerial energy," and that what was required was for managers at all levels in the public service to be "eager to maximise results, no longer frustrated or absolved from responsibility by central constraints, working with a sense of urgency to improve their service" (Jenkins, et al., 1988:16). In a subsequent critique, the Nuffield Institute argued that the "introduction of competition through the creation of an internal, or provider/purchaser market, and trading relationships between various agencies and service providers propels the NHS into largely uncharted waters and on a timescale which permits little opportunity for feedback and learning" (Harrison, et al., 1989:38). They assert that the proposed changes, "once embarked upon, could prove both *unpredictable and uncontrollable*" (Harrison, et al., 1989:38, italics added). In conclusion, the Nuffield describes the approach as one of "*controlled destabilisation* rather than *managed experimentation,*" and that the strategy carried major risks for the Government as well as substantial challenges for the NHS and its capacity to manage change without "flying apart at the seams" (Harrison, et al., 1988:38).

For Ferguson and Lavalette, the key turning point "was the passing of the *National Health Service and Community Care Act* 1990, based on a report by Sainsbury's managing director, Sir Roy Griffiths," which sought to introduce "market principles into health and social care, by changing the role of local authorities from providers of services to purchasers of services, based on competitive tendering by private and voluntary sector organisations" (2009). The implementation of this Act fundamentally changed the operation of social service departments and social work practice: "it spearheaded the establishment of the social work business through two inter-related developments - marketisation and managerialism" (Ferguson and Lavalette, 2009).

So, in essence, managerialism is primarily concerned with bringing the values and practices of private sector management –"in reality a wholly idealised and inaccurate version of these practices" (Ferguson and Lavalette, 2009)– into the public sector in general, and social work and social care in particular. As Ferguson and Lavalette explain, managers identify with the values of the *organisation*, rather than with "core social work values; re-fashioning clients as 'customers' and emphasising 'customer care,' in reality complaints procedures; an emphasis on 'performance review,' through inspectorates such as Ofsted; much tighter budgetary procedures, based on the view that efficient management, not increased resources, is the key to quality services; and 'clear leadership,' or in other words, stronger managerial structures" (2009).

Managerialism and the marketisation of social care simply don't work, and the attempt to run social services on business models has proved to be a disaster for social workers, social care workers and, of course, their clients. Social workers have less time to spend with clients, less time to consider and understand the problems their clients face, and fewer resources to deal with such problems.

Chris Jones and his colleagues ask the fundamental question: why should frontline social workers be controlled by highly paid managers who regard 'success' as meeting artificial performance indicators, and who pride themselves on managing budgets wholly inadequate to the needs of those who figure amongst the poorest and most disadvantaged in a deeply unequal society? And, additionally, on the issue of computerised technologies, he adds that these are "the people who amongst others are now orchestrating a huge data collection exercise as if the registration of the poorest will somehow allow the state to manage the growing problems of poverty and disadvantage" (2006). Jones et al. succinctly summarise social work and managerialism: "our work is shaped by managerialism, by the fragmentation of services, by financial restrictions and lack of resources, by increased bureaucracy and work-loads, by the domination of care-management approaches with their associated performance indicators and by the increased use of the private sector" (Jones et al., 2006).

These trends now dominate the day-to-day work of front line local authority social workers and therefore shape the welfare services offered to clients. The effect has been to increase the distance between managers and front line workers, and between social workers and clients. The main concern of too many social work managers is the control of budgets rather than the welfare of clients, while "worker-client relationships are increasingly characterised by control and supervision rather than care" (Jones, et al., 2006).

The 'choice' agenda

One of the consequences of the managerialist revolution in social work is that of *reducing the status of clients to that of consumers*. No longer are clients perceived to be passive recipients of services and, instead, are consumers. In place of a philosophy that holds that many *clients* are victims of deprivation and inequality, confused and in distress, whose individual behaviour has been shaped and reinforced by such disadvantage and who, indeed, may be *so damaged* they may not know exactly what they need and what may be available, *instead* –like individuals scouring the supermarket-they have *been re-configured as consumers,* knowing what their problems are and what 'service' is required to fix them. The assumption is that such consumers (clients) will drive up 'service quality' through competition for the consumer's patronage and encourage 'diversity of provision' to meet consumer preferences. Individuals are expected to make any choices 'responsibly' and to take greater levels of responsibility for their own well-being.

Clients have come to be both defined and described as whether or not they are able or prepared to 'engage' with social workers and social work intervention. In essence, this so-called 'modernisation agenda' challenges the collectivist principles of public welfare with, conversely, ideas of autonomy, choice, and personal responsibility (see Jordan, 2008).

Audit culture

The audit culture is now ingrained in public services. As Mary Douglas argues, the system we now inhabit is "almost ready to treat every death as chargeable to someone's account, every accident as caused by someone's criminal negligence, every sickness a threatened prosecution. Whose fault? is the first question"(1992:15-16). And as James Reason puts it, organisations typically respond to errors by "blaming and training," and invariably the implementation of tighter procedures (1995:171).

Processes are created which can be *audited* and if not followed *-even if they are incapable of being followed -* managers can then *apportion blame* and, as a consequence, public sentiment is placated. This audit culture is a familiar aspect of successive reforms across *all* public services: the determination to improve accountability through the micro-management of procedures, and the imposition of targets and performance indicators. All of these processes are invariably reliant on inflexible computerized information technologies.

It is perhaps in Social Services Departments where the audit culture has been most disastrous in its consequences. In other services, such as the NHS, the absurdities of 'targets' have been exposed. But while Government and successive inquiries have focused on 'flows of information' and how agencies -police, health, social workers- *communicate with one another*, the crucial central issue is ignored: *the complexity of emotional and interpersonal relationships*. For instance, what happens when a social worker sits in a room with a child and parent or carer -as one did with Peter Connelly two days before his death- and fails to notice anything amiss? What crucial skills does the social worker lack, or not use, which leads him or her to make such difficult judgments? *These are questions of personal development, experience, confidence: they do not fit neatly into public management tick boxes.*

The social and emotional complexities of social work

One of the observations that can be made is the extent to which many of the newly qualified social workers, and indeed second and third year students on placements, become involved in complex and emotionally demanding cases, (although this *tends* to occur more with the older, more 'mature' students).

A 40-year-old, newly qualified social worker, Jo, describes some of her work.

> I've had some really great cases that've had good *outcomes*. But I think the one that made me feel most proud of being a social worker was a mum with disabilities who'd previously

had her two children removed. 'Mum' was pregnant and because of previous removals, came straight to us. All the concerns from other professionals seemed to be around 'dad's' schizophrenia, despite the fact that actually he'd been well managed and been stable for six years and hadn't had a violent episode for some eleven years. He'd lost a daughter whilst he was in the psychiatric unit - you know, his then partner had had a child removed, which couldn't be attributed to him because he was within the psychiatric unit. It was a real uphill struggle for people to understand that actually, just because this chap had been labelled 'schizophrenic,' it didn't mean he was going to be a bad father.

There were lots of rumblings about this child being removed at birth, and not because of mum's lack of capability but to do with dad's label. And I really struggled, because I was a bit caught between the need to be really sure that I wasn't being blinded by my mental health hat -'please don't discriminate against him just because he's got a diagnosis'- and actually assessing what the risks were to this child. *I argued a lot with managers, team managers and with 'legal' and said actually, 'no, this baby needs to come home. We've not got enough risks to be saying that we need to be looking at another placement or removal at birth. It's just not there.'* And I was proved right. And actually she's since got back custody of her other two, and it's been fairly fairy tale! But I'm so pleased because I was only a year-and-a- half qualified at that point and I caused merry hell, but I wasn't prepared to back down. I'd done all number of risk assessments and made sure that I'd dotted every 'I' and crossed every 't,' to say, 'actually, look, we've no evidence' and I'm so pleased I did. I wasn't going to let legal push me around.

But Jo points out that social work intervention does not *always* go so well, or have such positive and fruitful outcomes.

I can think when I didn't shout loud enough. A 14-year-old lad, with chronic learning disability, came to our attention because he'd been raped and been found by his dad in this chap's house. He'd been there a couple of days, been raped anally and orally over a period of 48 hours. Quite how he'd not come to our attention before, I don't know, because it then transpired that when we talked to the school he'd been displaying really chronic sexualised behaviour and his parents weren't doing anything about it. And the reason he'd been with this chap who'd raped him was because he was out at two o'clock in the morning and his parents were very much, 'well, we can't fight with him, because he's physically a very big lad.' So the issue was, 'how do we protect this boy?' I was really concerned that I wasn't doing enough and I also thought 'these parents are being negligent in their duties, they're not doing *anything*.'

We then discovered through police investigations that he was *prostituting himself.* I was feeling a bit out of my league. I kept being told, 'no, we can't look at accommodation for this boy for his own protection.' I was like, 'yeah, but we've got procedures for kids who're within prostitution, he's got a learning disability there're all sorts of things, he's placing himself at risk *without knowing he's placing himself at risk, he has no understanding.*'

'Mum' wasn't so much in agreement, but 'dad' would have happily agreed for him to be accommodated to keep him safe. *My manager at the time said, 'no, you're over-reacting,' and he forbade me to have a conversation with legal and said, 'no, that's completely unreasonable, but you can take it to conference if you must.' And I didn't argue.*

Q. So what subsequently happened?

He's now in secure accommodation, because within about six months it became quite clear this boy *had* to be accommodated. I just thought if I'd really put my foot down and done this earlier and accommodated him earlier, could I have prevented, x,y and z? *It gave me sleepless nights.*

[Laughs] I nearly ran him over one night! I happened to be out in town and he ran right out in front of my car. Can you imagine the headline, 'Social Worker Kills Client!' But I thought if that hadn't have been *me* in the car, that could've been anybody driving 10 miles an hour faster than me, and this boy is running wild on the streets. *What was I doing as a social worker to stop it happening?*

Inequalities, deprivation and the social work client

Social and economic *inequalities* continue to blight the life-chances of huge numbers of individuals, families and communities. It's undeniable that there still exists a somewhat rigid social class system, with very little inter-generational mobility and, almost inevitably, a widening of the gap between rich and poor, the haves and have-not's. It is the working classes, the unemployed and disaffected classes who are the *primary* and *core* recipients of social work involvement. Social work tend not to be found on the 'playing fields of Eton and Fettes,' or indeed the 'classrooms and changing rooms of Roedean or Benenden.'

Ferguson and Lavalette provide one snapshot of the UK: communities riddled with drugs and drink and depression and stress; tens of thousands of young people abandoning their schools without any thought for the future; hundreds of thousands unskilled and alienated, with millions drained of hope and motivation. They argue that Government assumes that, nevertheless, by "flicking the switches of the benefits machine, these people can be manipulated into families or into work or out of crime as though they were carefully calculating their self-interest, as though their lives and sometimes their personalities had not been scrambled by the experience [of the last 20 years]" (2009). The consequence for social workers is that too often social workers are often doing little more than "supervising the deterioration of people's lives" (Jones, et al. 2006:2).

Just consider, for example, *educational inequality*:

- Approximately 2300 public schools (i.e., fee paying) educate an estimated 6 per cent of the population.

- A mere 253 of these schools belong to the association named the *Head Master's Conference,* and yet these schools account for 80 per cent of judges, 50 per cent of *senior* civil servants, and 75 per cent of bank directors.

- And, over 50 per cent of Oxbridge students have been educated at fee paying schools.

It is undeniable that money buys educational and therefore occupational *advantage* and, invariably, an increased sense of well-being, improved health and immediate access to high quality medicine, higher income and accumulated wealth. And, of course, such advantages are invariably passed on to the next generation.

Occupational inequalities also remain: for example, despite their variable and indeed debatable contribution to *societal* wealth and well-being, many in the financial sector are excessively rewarded in terms of income, assets and potential wealth, whereas those workers who *positively* contribute to societal well-being - nurses, teachers, social workers, dustmen and other public health workers- remain at a distinct disadvantage. Ferguson and Lavalette describe the *profound* inequalities that exist: a boy, "born in Hampstead,

London, will live around 11 years longer than a boy from St. Pancras, five stops away on London Underground's Northern Line." And, significantly, they also report that in "Strathclyde in the 1990's, for example, nine out of ten social work clients were in receipt of state benefits" (2009).

Consider the relationship between child abuse and poverty. Although, of course, the majority of poor parents do not abuse their children, where there *are* studies of the relationship *between class and child abuse*, they suggest a "clear link between poverty and maltreatment...[and, for example]...some 25 per cent of the children on the protection register in Coventry lived in just one electoral ward (the poorest in the city), although it only held 12 per cent of the city's children" (Ferguson and Lavalette, 2009).

In addition to the misery it creates in the lives of the sizeable minority, inequality is not actually beneficial to the *majority* of citizens either. Consider the statistical evidence and subsequent arguments of Wilkinson and Pickett in their seminal *The Spirit Level* (2009).

- In rich countries, a *smaller gap between rich and poor* means a happier, healthier, and more successful population. Just look at the US, the UK, Portugal, and New Zealand, compared to Japan, Norway or Sweden.

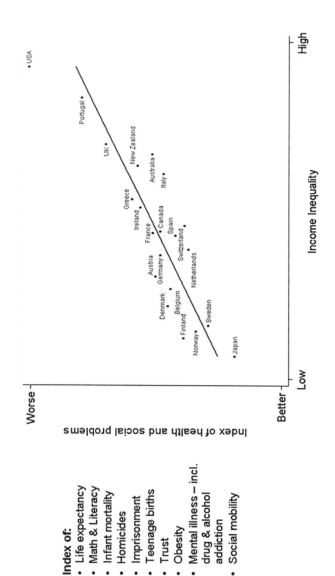

Health and Social Problems are Worse in More Unequal Countries

Index of:
- Life expectancy
- Math & Literacy
- Infant mortality
- Homicides
- Imprisonment
- Teenage births
- Trust
- Obesity
- Mental illness – incl. drug & alcohol addiction
- Social mobility

Source: Wilkinson & Pickett, The Spirit Level (2009)

www.equalitytrust.org.uk
™Equality Trust

- *More economic growth will not* lead to a happier, healthier, or more successful population. In fact, there's no relation between income per head and social well-being in rich countries.

- *If the UK were more equal,* the population would as a whole be better off. For example, the evidence suggests that if UK inequality was halved the murder rate *would also halve* and imprisonment would *reduce by 80 per* cent, and:

- - Teen births would *reduce by 80 per cent*
  - Mental illness would *reduce by two thirds*
  - Obesity would *halve.*

- *It's not just poor people who do better.* Wilkinson and Pickett's evidence suggests all people would benefit, although it's true that the poorest would gain the most.

Other social trends

- European nations face a demographic time bomb with *plunging birth rates* and an *ageing population* posing both a substantial threat to future economic prosperity and *profound challenges to public services*. A European Commission's *Green Paper on Demographic Change* asserts that from 2010 until 2030 the EU will lose 20.8 million (6.8 per cent) people of working age, and by 2030 will have 18 million fewer children and young people. In summary, there will only be two people of

working age for every person aged over
65 and over.

- The negative consequences of the over-
  sexualisation of children, partially created by
  the mass media including the advertising and
  merchandising industries. Early years teenage
  pregnancies and the rise in sexual crimes against
  women are two of the many possible consequences.

- The effects of globalisation, in terms of the pressure
  on public services through *additional and unplanned*
  increases in women of child-bearing age and of
  school age children. Interestingly -and perhaps
  absurdly- many Eastern European migrants
  work in child care and domestic labour while,
  simultaneously, leaving their *own* children back in
  their own homelands to be cared for by others.

- The decline and subsequent dismantling of the
  Soviet Union (1989-91) has resulted in an absence
  of *alternative social and economic models* to learn from
  and debate with.

- It has emerged that the state is compelled to step
  in when the greed and inefficiency in the private
  sector leads basic public services to the point of
  collapse, and its become apparent that only the state
  can guarantee the 'market,' which is regularly being
  'pulled out of shape' by some of its participants.

Social Workers

Social workers invariably come in all shapes and sizes, although predominantly from the working and lower-middle classes. But they *are* individuals, as are their clients. Robbie Gilligan describes the conundrum of trying to deal with *individual* problems through generic and inflexible systems: "Clients and their histories - are not administrative commodities to be accumulated and traded on computers or on hard copy files," their lives "cannot be comprehended, in all the senses of that word, in a set of case conference minutes, or the leaves of case files, or the full completion of a file template on a computer" (2004:99). The obverse is also true, that social workers should *not* be encouraged to act as *technicians*, formulaically responding to individual clients. Howe succinctly expresses the widely-held concern: "Practice no longer responds to the inherent meaning of the case, rather meaning is imposed according to the skills, resources and interests *of the organisation*" (1996:92, italics added). He adds that the relationships between the social worker and their clients "change from inter-personal to economic, from therapeutic to transactional, from nurturing and supportive to contractual and service oriented," and concludes that the *personal relationship* "once a central feature of social work practice is [now] stripped of its social, cultural, emotional and inter-personal dimension" (1996:92).

There are undoubtedly numerous problems with social work, perhaps especially social work in statutory settings. There are recruitment problems, there is a high sickness and absenteeism rate, there is the extensive and financially expensive use of agency staff, and there are questions of *morale*, hardly surprising given the continuing and relentless adverse media coverage the occupation is subject to. And perhaps any *increase* in the numbers of individuals wishing to undertake the social work degree shouldn't *necessarily* be seen as positive, as social work courses *may* be "prospering simply because they offer bursaries and fee remission" (Jones, et al., 2006:2).

Social work has become *deskilled* and this restructuring into so-called 'care management' has been described by some as the 'MacDonaldization of social work,' with workers being subjected to "increased control, surveillance and regulation" (Beresford, 2009). And, as a result of the Laming Inquiries, some commentators have begun to refer to social work as *merely* an 'informational sharing activity,' with the emphasis on the exchange of knowledge and perhaps not so much with *action*.

Beresford wryly notes that the "liberatory rhetoric of the International Federation of Social Workers, for example, 'striving for social justice, human rights and social development,' frequently seems risible next to the day to day role actually expected and required of social workers," and that often social work's workforce and its clients both experience it "*as a force for reaction and repression*" (2009).

Of the many reasons social work students cite for their career choice, a number are consistently repeated: a commitment to social justice; the desire to work with people; 'to make a difference'; and to use the experience of personal biography to help clients. Social work has *always* been driven by a *moral purpose* as well as that of *control*. There are *other* more pragmatic reasons for pursuing the career, as we've seen, and Reamer is dismayed by the apparent abandonment of traditional motivations: "a significant portion of the profession's members have abandoned their zeal for justice…in exchange for the pursuit of occupational security, enhanced status and income" (1992:11-12).

Social work tries to control those considered deviant or undesirable. And one of its other functions, unanticipated or otherwise, is to prevent widespread protest against social inequality and deprivation through attempting to deal with personal problems and thereby pacify such individuals. And, of course, bureaucratization, managerialism, cuts in resources, and occupational insecurity erode even further "the purposeful moral basis of good works and the good society" (Mullan, 1997:212).

Conclusions

The Task Force, in its lengthy deliberations, claims that it had "heard concerns that some people who would make excellent social workers might be excluded from social work training if the academic criteria are strengthened," and that it believed the answer "to this lies not in lowering capability requirements but in offering practical assistance and encouragement to suitable potential candidates in meeting the requirements for entry to the degree course" (2009:22). The Task Force adds that "exit routes to alternative, lower level or non-qualifying courses should be available in all programmes to enable those who are not competent or suitable to practise as social workers to complete a course in related areas," and also they "encourage [the] expansion of the Masters qualification for those who hold appropriate degrees" (2009:22). The Task Force's suggestions are wholly inappropriate. Many social work students study for the degree partly because they believe it to be an 'easy option,' with less of an emphasis on academic work and more on the practical side of the occupation, and others mistake social *work* for social *care*. Indeed, the central belief of the

Task Force appears to be that the solution to a client's problems is through *'better social workers.'*

Writing in 1959 about the *Younghusband Report* -the result of a government sponsored working party into statutory social work- economist Barbara Wootton argued that she actually believed social work to be an "untechnical [sic] job" with the only "specialist knowledge" required being that of an "encyclopaedic familiarity" with the various services and resources available (1959:254). She continued her somewhat caustic censure by arguing that the "saddest thing about the *Younghusband Report,* was that it shows not a glimmer of a conception of social work as a *self-liquidating profession"* (1959:261, italics added). Interestingly, Wootton believed that instead of social work making a contribution to the "partial elimination of social problems, managing more intractable ones and gradually phasing out its own activities," she foresaw an *expansion* of social work, with it becoming *less a means to an end and more an end in itself* (1959:262). She wasn't alone in her view about the unskilled nature of social work. For example, a study of newly qualified medical social workers in the 1960's found that "they spent between a third and a half of their time on work which did not require professional training either in their view or that of their heads of department" (Sinfield, 1969:22).

I've argued that social work has been deskilled; I've also argued that the root cause of social and individual distress is *societal.* I do not, of course, deny that certain individuals bear some responsibility for their travails. I do not believe that social work can in any sense be 'self-liquidating,' however, I *would* argue that the job does *not* require the training it hitherto has enjoyed and what is proposed for the future.

The research: a recap.

Let us remind ourselves of the main findings from the interviews with students and newly qualified social workers. What might we learn from *their* perception of education, training and practice?

Students entered social work, predominantly, after a life of childhood disturbance, emotional uncertainty, the sense of loss and an equal sense of 'not belonging,' and, also and importantly, a desire to help others, 'make a difference,' and perhaps to somehow combat social injustice.

The students interviewed conformed to the national profile: increasingly younger candidates, very few *men* and very few individuals of either gender from ethnic minority backgrounds. There was a consensus that many students are too young to train and graduate as social workers, and that such graduates would be unable to perform on appointment at the appropriate level. The *majority* opinion was that clients would prefer social workers who had endured more of a substantial and varied life experience, and perhaps even parented children of their own.

Unsurprisingly -given the diminution of serious political discourse and behaviour of parliamentarians- the students were not particularly *political*. Interestingly, the widespread opinion among students was that their *emotional intelligence and personalities* were not sufficiently considered or developed. It was widely asserted that between 5 to 10 per cent of fellow students were *unfit to practice* as social workers.

Many students found modules either too intellectually demanding *or* too simple. A recurrent theme was that there was a surfeit of social science subjects, yet insufficient coverage of both child and adult protection. In terms of teaching skills and module organization, there was a general sense of a preference for *interaction* in the classroom, including teaching through seminars. Unsurprisingly, there were variations in opinion about individual tutors and the efficacy or otherwise of tutorial help.

The students responded fully and comprehensively to questions about their practical placements. What emerges includes deep disquiet over the administration of placements, especially the way in which student requests failed to be met. Many of the placements were perceived *not* to be social work opportunities but, rather, unpaid labour in social *care* settings. The student perception of social work varied, although there appeared to be a consensus that *statutory* social work was not necessarily 'real' social work.

Many students expressed the opinion that the degree was insufficiently *practical*, and that they felt they'd benefit from practical-related learning at university, like report writing and administrative formats. Some students considered the degree to be "too easy" and, unsurprisingly, a number of them believed that recruitment would increase if the course length was substantially reduced. Students argued that the social work degree, with its substantial practical component, requires a commitment that may create or exacerbate both familial and financial difficulties.

A number of participants expressed the view that social work was even *more* complex and challenging than they'd originally imagined. Some students questioned whether it could actually be *taught* and that perhaps an individual had to be inherently or innately hard-wired for the job. Students expressed disquiet at publicly discussing their chosen occupation, acutely aware of the widespread condemnation of social work. However, there was the potentially positive belief that the current period was a 'watershed moment' for the development of social work.

The *newly qualified social workers* repeated many of the student opinions. For example, there was frustration at the extensive and ever-increasing bureaucratization involved in practice. Similarly, both the target culture and the predominance of managerial oversight were widely spoken of in disparaging terms. Many workers spoke about "real social work," when criticizing the deskilled role of care management.

The newly qualified social workers were fairly unanimous in the opinion that the degree course did not equip them for frontline work in either child or adult protection. They also believed that students on the degree would benefit from there being more teaching about the various bureaucratic and computer *systems* they'd encounter in the field.

Again, in symmetry with the students, the newly qualified workers valued the idea of multidisciplinary or interprofessional working, but argued that whether or not such working was effective or positive was dependent on the *individuals* involved and, additionally, that certain professional cultures were more amenable to shared work than others.

Post-qualifying education was neither welcomed nor considered to be valuable.

The Social Work Reform Board

Since 2009-10, the Social Work Reform Board (SWRB) and its working groups have attempted to develop the Social Work Task Force's (SWTF) recommendations and have involved "social workers, service users and carers, managers, senior leaders and educators in their design" (SWRB, 2010:14). In a vein similar to that of the culture of the English civil service -much discussion and generation of paperwork by the 'great and the good,' followed by further discussion- the Reform Board has spent considerable time in the production of very little of substance.

Of the fifteen recommendations previously made by the Task Force, five have been developed by the Reform Board. They are: an overarching professional standards framework; standards for employers and a supervision framework; principles that should underpin a continuing professional development framework; proposed requirements for social work education – "so that student social workers receive high quality preparation for joining the profession"; and proposals for effective partnership working (2010:14-15).

Furthermore, the Reform Board proposes that the core themes of the 'overarching professional standards framework,' which "underpin the whole social work reform programme," should be: *Professionalism*: "Identify and behave as a professional social worker," (2010:14) committed to professional development. *Values and Ethics*: Apply social work ethical principles and values to guide professional practice. *Diversity*: Recognise diversity and apply anti-discriminatory and anti-oppressive principles in practice. *Rights, Justice and Economic Wellbeing*: "*Advance human rights, and promote social justice and economic well-being*" (2010:14, italics added). *Knowledge*: Apply knowledge of social sciences, law and social work practice theory. *Critical Reflection and Analysis*: Apply critical reflection and analysis to inform and provide a rationale for professional decision-making. *Intervention and Skills*: "Use judgement and authority to intervene with individuals, families and *communities*" (2010:14, italics added) to promote independence, provide support and prevent harm, neglect and abuse. *Contexts and Organisations*: Engage with, inform, and adapt to changing contexts that shape practice. Operate effectively within own organisational frameworks and contribute to the

development of services and organisations. "Operate
effectively within multi-agency and inter-professional
settings" (2010:15). And, finally, *Professional Leadership*:
Take responsibility for the professional learning and
development of others through "supervision, mentoring,
assessing, research, teaching, leadership and management"
(2010:15, italics added).

Despite the hundreds of thousands of hours expended by
the many participants -the members of the Reform Board,
"social workers, service users and carers, managers, senior
leaders and educators"- in producing this "overarching
professional standards framework," the end result is
profoundly disappointing. *Any course from any institution
from the past five decades would have repeated a similar check
list.* And, depressingly, such lists would have contained the
same unsustainable, ill-defined and unrealistic analyses,
assertions and targets. For example, how precisely is the
social worker meant to "advance human rights" and
"promote social justice and economic well-being"? Are
they expected to campaign for the rights of asylum seekers
and women in the workplace, at the same time as lobbying
Parliament for an end to child poverty and demonstrating
against the profits of UK retailers who rely on international
child labour? Similarly, how do social workers intervene
in "communities"? What *precisely* does this mean? And,
finally, in which pressurised hour of the day is the social
worker expected to "assess, research and teach" in order to
demonstrate their "professional leadership"?

In terms of social work *education*, the Reform Board
proposes that there should be "more rigorous selection
criteria, standards for practice educators, an integrated
curriculum framework based on the overarching professional
standards framework, the consistent and substantive

involvement of service users and carers in the design and delivery of courses, and transparent, targeted and effective regulation" (2010:16).

A cursory examination of the Reform Board's *more detailed 'evidence-based recommendations'* is further indicative of the paucity of the Reform Board's work. Within the section, 'the proposals for improving the calibre of entrants to social work degrees' (2010a:49-52), the Board proposes new guidelines for individual interviews and group activities. In respect of the former, the Board asserts that "*all* candidates who are finally selected for the social work degree should have performed well in an individual interview to evaluate their communication skills, commitment, understanding of social work, and life and work experience" (2010a:51). However, such decisiveness is immediately followed by a caveat:"There is mixed research evidence of the effectiveness of interviews as a selection method and some HEIs have stopped undertaking interviews for reasons of cost and time. However, except for a small proportion of academics, *there is a strong intuitive view*, that all applicants should be interviewed due to the importance of good communication and relationship building skills for effective social work practice" (2010a:51, italics added). And on group activities, the Board argues that "*all* candidates should participate successfully in a group activity/exercise prior to acceptance onto the course," and while the value of these is recognised, "in the current funding environment it is proposed that the method should be left to the discretion of each HEI based on resource and capacity issues" (2010a: 51). So, *which* method? How is "success" to be measured in terms of an applicant's participation? And what if the HEI's "resource and capacity" problems mean that there can be *no* group activities: does that mean that they will a priori be recruiting fewer able students? Indeed, what are the implications for the administration of *individual* interviews in an era of economic decline and HEI contraction?

Another piece of work in the same paradigm as that of the Reform Board is that of the *The Munro Review of Child Protection*. It originates from 10 June 2010, when the Secretary of State for Education commissioned Professor Eileen Munro of the London School of Economics to conduct a wide-ranging independent review to improve child protection. And on 10 May 2011, she published her final report *in which* she makes fifteen recommendations, aimed at more adequately preparing social work students for the challenges of child protection work. She argues that the work of the Social Work Task Force and the Social Work Reform Board should be built upon to improve 'frontline expertise' (2011:85). From 2011 onwards and in consultation with various 'professionals,' Professor Munro's report will be subject to ministerial scrutiny.

The Munro Review argues that the 'requisite expertise' for child and family social work consists of three elements: (i) relationship skills; (ii) reasoning and emotions in relationship-based practice; and (iii) using evidence (2011:91). The *Review* adds that the Social Work Reform Board is "leading work to develop a Professional Capabilities Framework" (2011:98). This, she asserts, aims to "set out clearly" what is expected in terms of a social worker's knowledge, skills and capacity and how they build over time as they move through their careers. Munro states that she "believes that an important early step for the Professional Capabilities Framework is to set out the capabilities necessary for effective practice in child and family social work" (2011:98), and "strongly endorses" the capabilities on professionalism; values and ethics; diversity; rights, justice and economic wellbeing; contexts and organisations; and professional leadership. And on practical placements, she *recommends* that Higher Education Institutions (HEIs) and employing agencies should "work together" (don't they do so already?) so that "practice placements are of the *highest quality*" (2011:101, italics added). Does she believe that HEIs and employing agencies try *not* to provide "high quality" placements, that they are content with providing inadequate placements? Perhaps, a more accurate prediction is to acknowledge that in a context of economic decline and lack of growth combined with uncertainty in higher education, it is unlikely that nothing of substance will emerge.

Recommendations

Much of social work is reasonably effective, competent and certainly courageous, but many of the problems social workers deal with are *socially created* and the solutions are, unsurprisingly, *social and economic.* Additionally, many of these problems are *perennial*: as social work doyen, Helen Harris Perlman, puts it, many of the "problems social workers deal with are as old as original sin" (1989: 12). My agenda is as follows:

- *Inequality* has to be perceived as a root cause of personal problems and public issues, and appropriately addressed. Simply consider two aspects of inequality and disadvantage: *Life expectancy* data for the UK in 2011 reveals a north-south divide in terms of death, of four-years. The data from the Office for National Statistics shows that for men in the south-east of England it is 79.4 years, while in Scotland the figure is 75.4. For women the gap is slightly less: 83.3 in south-east and south-west England, against 80.1 in Scotland. The areas with lowest life expectancy are Greater Glasgow and Clyde (which has a lower rate than Albania for men), Hartlepool, the Western Isles, Liverpool and Blackburn. The pattern remains similar to those of previous years, demonstrating just how stubborn social and economic inequalities remain (*Guardian,* 2011, June 8). Similarly, in 2011, hundreds of thousands of older people in England who need social care are not getting any support from the state or private sector. Age UK reports that 800,000 people are excluded from the system - and the figure is set to top one million within four years. Budgets had hardly risen in recent years even before the squeeze, despite the ageing population, and additionally, councils have also been making it more difficult for those who do meet the income threshold to get care, by tightening the eligibility criteria. In 2005, half of councils provided support to people with 'moderate needs,' but in 2011 that figure had dropped to 18%. The Age UK report pointed out while the NHS had received significant budget rises in recent years, social care increases had stalled (Triggle, 2011).

- Jones et al., discussing the growth in international anti-capitalist global protest movements, argue that such movements and the debates they engage in, "can help us think about the shape of a modern engaged social work based around such 'anti-capitalist' values as democracy, solidarity, accountability, participation, justice, equality, liberty and diversity" (Jones, et al., 2009:3).

- Social work has to resist further fragmentation. Social work has *always* worked with a variety of diverse client groups. As Beresford argues, if social work is to retain its critical mass and solidarity, it is important that there's a "united fight back against the regressive pressures it faces, across different forms of social work and social work with different groups." He adds that it was "unlikely to be helpful for social work with children and families to try and campaign alone" (2009).

- Social work must be committed to *trade unionism* – organisations, a political leadership and an ideology representative of labour, not capital. And trade unionism is where social work 'leadership' should be generated. More than any other Welfare State occupation, social work seeks to understand the links between 'public issues' and 'private troubles' and seeks to address both. It is for this reason that "many who hold power and influence in our society would be delighted to see a demoralised and defeated social work, a social work that is incapable of drawing attention to the miseries and difficulties which beset so many in our society" (Jones et al., 2006).

- *Students should be admitted to degree courses on the basis of a transparent and somehow demonstrable commitment to social justice.*

- Student work-based learning should include either a residential or community placement *in addition* to those in the field. The length of time should not be decreased, but increased.

- Much of the social science content of degree courses should be eliminated. Clients require social workers well-acquainted with the availability of resources and agency procedures, and inter-personal sensitivity, *not* social scientific conundrums – however inherently interesting or intellectually demanding. Of course, many social work educators might well disagree with many of my arguments and recommendations, not least because it is in their employment prospects to do so. Indeed, writing as a sociologist recommending the diminution of such teaching on the social work degree, I perfectly understand the sentiment. With Comte, I too consider sociology to be the 'Queen of the social sciences' dealing, as it does, with the wide-ranging and complex issues of the social world and incorporating many other intellectual disciplines as it does so. But to continue the teaching of sociology on the social work degree in an *unquestioning manner* would be performing an injustice both to sociology and the needs of the student. Recommendations such as reducing the input of sociology on the degree course may well of course appeal to those politicians and administrators who decry social science, but I would be cowardly to ignore my observations and conclusions.

- There's little need for students to be intellectually assaulted by vacuous pseudo-social work theories. Biestek's 1959 model (in *The Casework Relationship*) provides a clear and coherent framework for any inter-personal work, following the principles of individualization, purposeful expression of feelings, controlled emotional involvement, acceptance, the non-judgemental attitude, client self-determination, and confidentiality (Biestek, 1959). Once incorrectly derided as being opposed to socially or politically-based social work and, instead, being merely a handbook for individual analysis, the perception has come full circle. The book provides a respectful basis for so-called relational work within the context of the requirement of *social change.*

- Dissertation and research writing should be eliminated and replaced by *community profiling*, whereby students observe and learn about the communities they work in and discover the extent of deprivation -in health, housing, income, policing and education- that their potential clients endure.

- More academic time should be spent on applied and practical issues and processes: for example, more work on child and adult protection, report writing, court protocols and organizational cultures.

- Given that many clients suffer and endure problems due to the lack of a father in their or their children's lives, or have insufficient income to provide for their children, students should learn more about and discuss in more detail (using case study material) human sexuality, sexual behaviour and interventions within sexual behaviour, such as the various types of contraception, terminations and the psychological, social and economic issues involved in procreation.

This final *student account* of practical training perhaps illuminates much of what has been argued.

Nigel, 31, a final year student, begins by highlighting what he sees as a power imbalance.

The placements are only as good as you make them, but crucially also only as good as they allow you to be. *You have no power.* You are powerless from what you choose [on PIMS] to what you can do in there. My first placement was in a local charity for learning disability. I was the first student there so I walked in and spent two weeks thinking, 'what the fucking hell am I going to do?' But it was actually a good learning thing for me because I learnt how to engage with people. It was a very structured setting for people with learning disability and I challenged that structure in that, you know what, '*these are people.*' It was all about work and I said, 'would you want to work if you had enough money - would you want to work?'

Q. I gather you have strong opinions about the particular tutor whose job it is to source and arrange placements?

The tutor in charge of placements held
a lecture on practice organising and he is
fucking rude, he is very, very arrogant and not
approachable. *My opinion.* I am not suggesting
for a second that his job's not hard, but you
know what, my placement is hard. *Do your
job.* Because he has a choice, he can leave if
he really wants to. *I can't,* he's put me in a
placement where I am fucking stuck.

*From my experience so far -and it's been pretty
limited- social work is not done in statutory
organisations.* In fact I would probably go so far
as to say that I did loads of social work in my
first placement in a charity. *Statutory social work
is a pen-pushing exercise and you know, I am in it,
that's what I'm doing and I'm a hypocrite because I'll
soon be starting a job in it because I need the money.*

Interesting social worker roles have now
dropped the social work title because they've
become aligned to the fact that people don't
like this, they don't like what it stands for and
you're now called different things.

Q. Ok. Tell me about your current placement.

My current placement's at CAFCASS, the
Court Advisory Support System. If you want
to torture someone, just put them there. If
you want to teach empowerment or *lack of
power,* put someone there. I knew I was going
to get a statutory placement and I knew it'd

be children because of the way the university
works in terms of adult placement one year,
children the next. I disagree with that – *where
is the choice*? Where's the drive to help people
find something they're interested in?

I'm in a position where I'm in with a newly
qualified member of staff, in a job.   Then,
as things unfold, I am struggling with the
computer system. There're only two stand
alone computers in the whole place, the rest
are lap tops and they're designated for people
and bank staff so I couldn't get on any of
the computers. They're minor issues. But,
I'm working in an atmosphere of people just
stressing out.

I'm not naïve. But, later I find out that
actually I've been put into a placement where
a woman was stabbed and killed. That was
one of the cases at CAFCASS and it's one of
the reasons there's a 100-case backlog. This is
a place where there's been nine managers in
the last 18 months and currently no manager.
The building was 'Ofsteded' as *unfit for practice*.
There's no fire officer there, no first aider.

Nigel describes problems of education and training, and
problems in practice. Social work is too important for
any shortcomings in its training and in its practice to be
ignored. The support and intervention of social workers
is essential in societies based on inequality and in which
many individuals also face problems in relationships and

parenting. Social workers need to be socially and politically committed, appropriately trained and properly valued. The Task Force's agenda may well raise the status and perhaps the employment prospects of individual social workers, and it may well raise their profile through the establishment of a professional body, *but it will not address the major issue of the root cause of personal and public distress, or the recruitment and training of students, and nor will it positively re-configure the job.* Social work should be dealing with individuals, in a personal and individual manner, always acutely aware of the *social and economic context* of personal problems.

Bibliography

Banks, Sarah (2006) *Ethics and Values in Social Work*, Palgrave: London.

Beresford, Peter (2009), posted on *Social Work Future*, April 12.

Biestek, Felix (1959) *The Casework Relationship*, University of Chicago Press: Illinois.

Brake, Mike and Bailey, Roy eds. (1980) *Radical Social Work Practice*, Edward Arnold: London.

Brandon, Marian (2009) Personal communication, 14 May 2009.

Braverman, Harry (1974) *Labor and Monopoly Capital: The Degradation of Work in the Twentieth Century*, Monthly Review Press: New York.

Bryman, Alan (2008) *Social Research Methods*, 3rd edition, Oxford University Press: Oxford.

Carey, Malcolm (2009) 'Happy Shopper? The Problem with Service User and Carer Participation,' *British Journal of Social Work*, Volume 39, pp. 179-188.

Community Care, Media Monitor, 12 May 2009.

Department of Health (2002) *Requirements for Social Work Training*, HMSO: London.

Department of Health, Personal communication, 3 June 2009.

Department of Health, Letter from Andy Burnham and Ed Balls, 1 December 2009.

Dominelli, L. (2002) 'Anti-oppressive practice in context', in Adams, R., Dominelli, L. and Payne, M. (eds) *Social Work: Themes, Issues and Critical Debates* (2nd edition), Palgrave: Basingstoke.

Douglas, Mary (1992) *Risk and Blame: Essays in Cultural Theory*, Sage: London.

Ferguson, Iain and Lavalette, Michael (2009) 'Social Work After "Baby P",' on SWAN [Social Work Action Network] web site.

Gilligan, Robbie (2004) 'Promoting resilience in child and family social work: issues for social work practice, education and policy,' *Social Work Education*, Volume 23(1), pp. 93 – 104.

Goleman, Daniel (1996) *Emotional Intelligence*, Bloomsbury: London.

Guardian (2011) *DataBlog*, June 8.

Harrison, Stephen, Hunter, David J., Johnston, Ian, and Wistow, Gerald (1989) *Competing for Health: A Commentary on the NHS Review*, The Nuffield Institute: University of Leeds.

Holmstrom, Cath and Taylor, Imogen (2008) 'Researching Admissions: What Can We Learn about Selection of Applicants from Findings about Students in Difficulty on a Social Work Programme?' *Social Work Education*, Vol 17 (8), December, pp.819-836.

Howe, David (1996) 'Surface and depth in social-work practice,' pp. 77-97 in Parton, Nigel ed. (1996) *Social Theory, Social Change and Social Work*, Routledge: London.

Jack, Gordon and Donnellan, Helen (2010) 'Recognising the person within the Developing Professional: Tracking the Early Careers of Newly Qualified Child Care Workers in Three Local Authorities in England', *Social Work Education*, Vol.29, No.3, April, pp.305-318.

Jenkins, Kate, Caines, Karen and Jackson, Andrew (1988) *Improving Management in Government: The Next Steps*, HMSO: London.

Jones, Chris et al. (2006) 'The Good Fight,' *Guardian,* March 16 2006.

Jordan, Bill (2008) *Welfare and Well-being: Social Value in Public Policy*, Policy Press: Bristol.

Kuhn, Thomas H. (1962) *The Structure of Scientific Revolutions*, University of Chicago Press: Chicago.

Laing, R.D. and Esterson, A. (1964) *Sanity, Madness and the Family*, Tavistock Publications: London.

MacKay, K. and Woodward, R. (2010) 'Exploring the place of values in the new social work degree in Scotland,' *Social Work Education*, Volume 29(6), pp.633-45.

Mahadevan, Janaki (2009) 'Male social work recruitment falls for third year,' *Children and Young People Now,* February 4.

Mayer, John and Timms, Noel (1970) *The Client Speaks*, Routledge and Kegan Paul: London

Moriarty, Jo and Murray, Jo (2007) 'Who Wants to be a Social Worker? Using Routine Published Data to Identify Trends in the Numbers of People Applying for and Completing Social Work Programmes in England,' *British Journal of Social Work*, Vol 37, pp. 715-33.

Mullan, Bob (1995) *Mad to be Normal: Conversations with RD Laing*, Free Association Books: London.

Mullan, Bob (1997) *Modern Social Work in Search of a Soul: Felix Biestek, In the Service of Others*, ISP: San Francisco.

Munro, Eileen (2011) *The Munro review of Child Protection: Final Report*, HMSO: London.

Orme, J. et al (2009) 'What (a) Difference a Degree Makes: The Evaluation of the New Social Work Degree in England,' *British Journal of Social Work*, Vol 39, pp. 161-178.

Parton, Nigel (2001) 'The current state of social work in UK universities: some personal reflections,' *Social Work Education*, Volume 20 (2), pp.167-174.

Parton, Nigel. ed (1996) *Social Theory, Social Change and Social Work*, Routledge: London.

Perlman, Helen Harris (1989) *Looking Back to See Ahead*, University of Chicago Press: Chicago.

Pithouse, David et al (2009) 'A Tale of Two CAFs: The Impact of the Electronic Common Assessment Framework,' *British Journal of Social Work*, Volume 39, pp.599-612.

QAA (2007) Code of Practice for the assurance of academic quality and standards in higher education. Section 9: Work-based and placement learning – September 2007.

Reamer, Frederic G. (1992) 'Social Work and the Public Good: Calling or Career?' pp.11-33, in Reid, Nelson and Popple, Philip eds (1992) *The Moral Purposes of Social Work*, Nelson-Hall: Chicago.

Reason, J. (1995) *Comprehensive Error Management in Aircraft Engineering*, BAE: London.

SCIE, Personal Communication, 21 May, 2009.

Shaw, I. et al. (2009) 'An Exemplary Scheme? An Evaluation of the Integrated Children's System,' *British Journal of Social Work*, Volume 39, pp.613-626.

Social Work Task Force (2009) *Building a safe, confident future: The final report of the Social Work Task Force,* November 2009: London.

Social Work Reform Board (2010) *Building a safe and confident future: one year on (summary document)*, SWRB: London.

Social Work Reform Board (2010a) *Building a safe and confident future: one year on (detailed document)*, SWRB: London.

Swingewood, Alan (2000) *A Short History of Sociological Thought*, 3rd edition, Palgrave: London.

Triggle, Nick (2011) '800,000 not given help with social care,' BBC News *Health*, May 30.

Vincent, Jane (1996) 'Why ever do we do it? Unconscious motivation in choosing social work as a career,' *Journal of Social Work Practice*, Vol 10 (1), pp.63-69.

Weber, Max (1948) in Gerth, H. and Mills, C. Wright (eds) *From Max and Weber*, Routledge and Kegan Paul: London.

Wootton, Barbara (1959) 'Daddy Knows Best,' *The Twentieth Century,* Volume 166, pp.248-61.